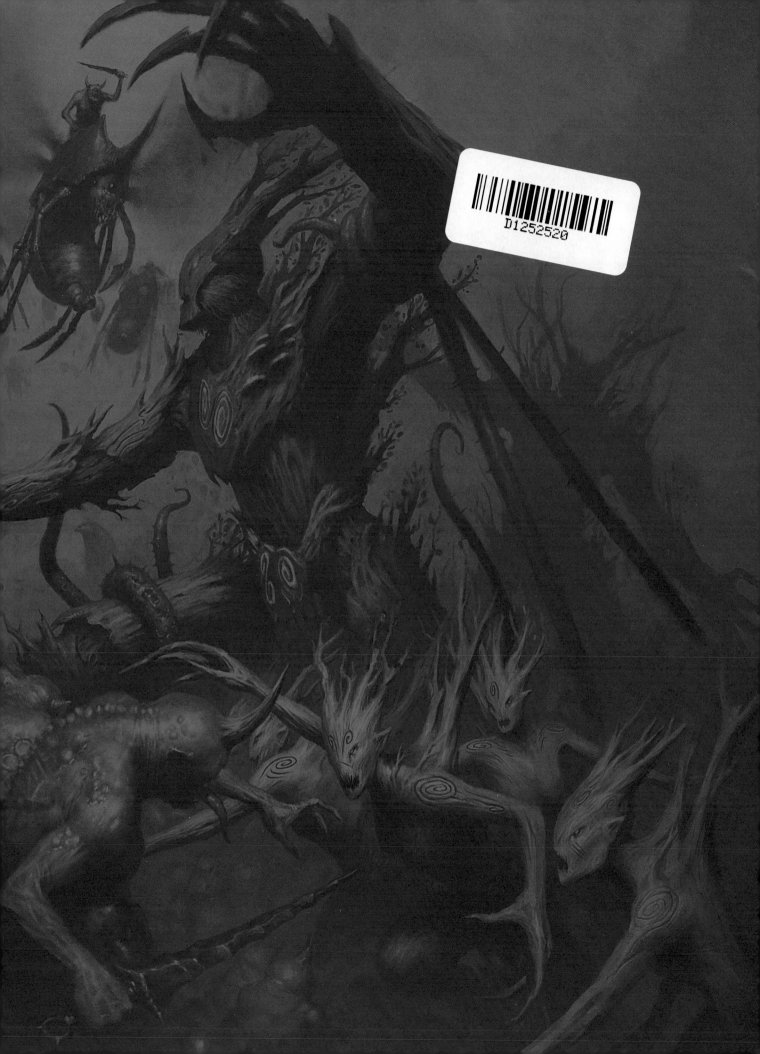

From the maelstrom of a sundered world, the Eight Realms were born. The formless and the divine exploded into life. Strange, new worlds appeared in the firmament, each one gilded with spirits, gods and men. Noblest of the gods was Sigmar. For years beyond reckoning he illuminated the realms, wreathed in light and majesty as he carved out his reign. His strength was the power of thunder. His wisdom was infinite. Mortal and immortal alike kneeled before his lofty throne. Great empires rose and, for a while, treachery was banished. Sigmar claimed the land and sky as his own and ruled over a glorious age of myth.

But cruelty is tenacious. As had been foreseen, the great alliance of gods and men tore itself apart. Myth and legend crumbled into Chaos. Darkness flooded the realms. Torture, slavery and fear replaced the glory that came before. Sigmar turned his back on the mortal kingdoms, disgusted by their fate. He fixed his gaze instead on the remains of the world he had lost long ago, brooding over its charred core, searching endlessly for a sign of hope. And then, in the dark heat of his rage, he caught a glimpse of something magnificent. He pictured a weapon born of the heavens. A beacon powerful enough to pierce the endless night. An army hewn from everything he had lost. Sigmar set his artisans to work and for long ages they toiled, striving to harness the power of the stars. As Sigmar's great work neared completion, he turned back to the realms and saw that the dominion of Chaos was almost complete. The hour for vengeance had come. Finally, with lightning blazing across his brow, he stepped forth to unleash his creation.

The Age of Sigmar had begun.

CONTENTS

DESIGNED BY GAMES WORKSHOP IN NOTTINGHAM
With thanks to The Faithful for their additional playtesting services.

GRANDFATHER NURGLE

Nurgle is the Chaos God of plagues, whose power waxes strong when disease and despair ravage the Mortal Realms. Though he is a source of fear and revulsion to his enemies, Nurgle is a perversely paternal god, generous with his foul gifts and proud of his worshippers' every disgusting achievement.

Nurgle wishes to see rot and contagion bloom across the Mortal Realms, drowning the bastions of his enemies in a tide of putrid filth. Yet Nurgle is not malicious – far from it. The Plague God delights in fecundity, and the overabundance of life that disease and decay brings. To Nurgle, every raddled corpse is a welcoming nursery for wriggling maggots and cloying plague spores. Every stagnant lake and rotting forest is a paradise in which parasitic larvae and bountiful poxes can flourish. These are the gifts that Nurgle lavishes upon the Mortal Realms, and if there is malice behind his generosity it is directed only at those ingrates who try to decline his offerings.

Nurgle's physical aspect is truly hideous. He is a swollen mountain of blubber and pus, whose necrotic flesh crawls with buboes and seethes with lice. Filth and foulness drool from the rotting maws that dot his corpulent mass, and flies the size of boulders buzz around him in thick clouds, drawn by his stench.

Since time immemorial, Nurgle has been in competition with his siblings, the other Dark Gods. In their great game, Nurgle is typically ranked third most powerful behind wrathful Khorne and duplicitous Tzeentch. Yet this is a misleading notion, for in truth Nurgle is in no way inferior to his brothers.

Rather, his might surges and recedes in a never-ending cycle. When plague and pestilence run rampant, Nurgle becomes so swollen with power that his leathery hide struggles to contain it. When remission comes, and Nurgle's plagues fall fallow, so his power wanes until he becomes a hollowed out shadow of his former greatness. Yet Nurgle is never defeated for long, for disease and decay are as inevitable as time and tide.

Nurgle has a far less fraternal relationship with the Horned Rat, the verminous Skaven deity who joined the Chaos pantheon at the fall of the world-that-was. As an architect of plague and pestilence, the horned Rat seems a natural ally of Nurgle, and certainly the two gods find common cause on occasion. Yet where Nurgle wishes to spread bilious life, the Horned Rat seeks only the ruin of all, with

no thought for new life or creation. As a result, Nurgle looks down on the vermin-god as short-sighted and distasteful, more of a means to an end than a true ally.

When the Age of Chaos began, Nurgle set his sights upon the inexhaustible cornucopia of Ghyran. His armies spilled across the Jade Kingdoms, corrupting everything in their path. Thousands of mortal tribes turned to Nurgle's worship in order to save themselves from his countless plagues. The sylvaneth and their queen, Alarielle, were driven into hiding, and for a time Nurgle stood upon the very cusp of victory. Yet at the last, an alliance between Sigmar's Stormcast Eternals and the resurgent sylvaneth defeated Nurgle's greatest champions. Alarielle sealed the Genesis Gate, through which the greatest portion of Nurgle's might had flowed into Ghyran.

For a time, Nurgle wallowed in the despondency of rejection, and as he did so his armies were driven back on every front. But now the Plague God's optimism has returned, and with it the realisation that – in obsessing over the conquest of Ghyran – he was being selfish. All of the Mortal Realms deserve to benefit from Nurgle's generosity, and he means to make sure that they are all showered with his blessings until they can take no more…

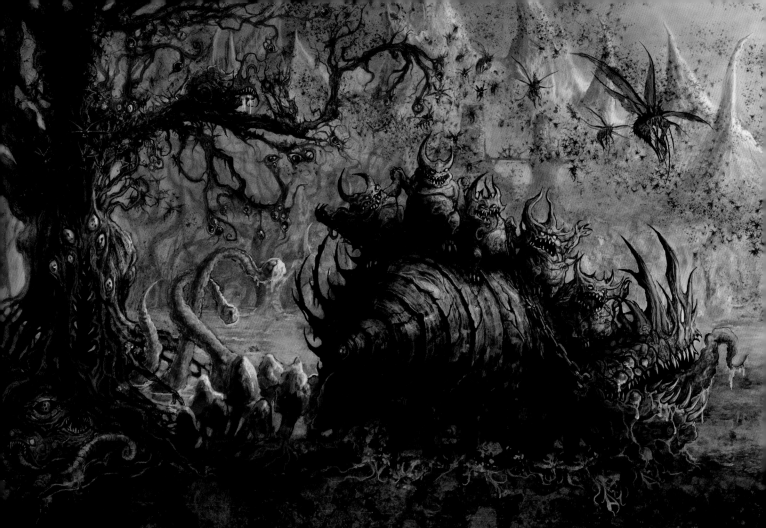

THE GARDEN OF NURGLE

The Garden of Nurgle is the Plague God's domain within the Realm of Chaos. It is a festering amalgam of jungle, forest, swamp and ornamental parkland in which unclean life seethes, and sickness blossoms with epidemic intensity.

No living being save a worshipper of Nurgle could hope to survive within the Plague God's garden. Its winding paths run with diseased slurry and squirming worms, while the air is thick with miasmal fumes and the constant drone of flies unnumbered. Groves of Feculent Gnarlmaws jostle with bloated fungi and stinking fever-blooms. Sickly light spills from floating spore-sacs that drift through the murk, trailing slimy lianas with pus-fat thorns. Everywhere mucus drips, insects scuttle, and nauseating gases bubble and pop. Fountains of mouldering bone rise from congealed lakes, jetting putrid slop from squealing sphincters. Meadows of grass like rusted blades creak and groan in the languid breeze, spewing clouds of seeds that would rot mortal flesh in seconds.

As Nurgle's power ebbs and flows, so the boundaries of his garden realm expand and contract. When his might is at its peak, the Garden of Nurgle bursts its existential bounds and surges into the territories of the other Chaos Gods. Plains of fire-blackened skulls and fractal crystal mazes are swiftly overrun by the garden's predatory fecundity, turning all to bountiful filth.

The Chaos Gods are ever at war, for they fight as only immortal brothers can. Each maintains countless armies of daemonic soldiery with which to defend their own domains, while invading those of their brothers. Nurgle is no exception to this trend, and his garden teems with the commanders and foot soldiers of his daemon legions. Patrol bands of Plague Drones thrum along the garden's myriad paths, seeking invaders to torment. Tides of diminutive Nurglings scamper through the foetid underbrush intent on mischief, while packs of slug-like Beasts of Nurgle slither and lollop amidst the

marshy pools searching for unfortunate playmates. Fortresses and guard towers of rancid blubber and corroded iron loom over seeping gallows-trees, garrisoned by Plaguebearers who watch for hardy interlopers to punish.

At the heart of the garden stands Nurgle's Manse. The Dark God lumbers about this suppurating fastness, whistling phlegm-thick tunes as he gathers ingredients for his latest plague. Each new malady is brewed to perfection in his immense cauldron and then tested on the cursed creature known as the Poxfulcrum, a caged being that has endured millennia of misery as Nurgle's personal test bed. Only once he is satisfied with the results of his concoction does Nurgle upend the cauldron, raining new contagions down upon the Mortal Realms.

'In the middle distance I saw a great fortress, half hidden by the miasma of decay that infused its very structure. Rotten and mildewed were its timbers, and its sagging roof was thick with infestation of every conceivable kind. Poison poured down the walls of this most revolting of abodes, polluting everything about. Yet despite its state of decay, I sensed an inevitability about that unhallowed bastion. I knew beyond doubt that it had stood for years uncounting in that same ramshackle form, and would continue on until the very end of time.

Before the fortress gates stretched a forest of death. Corpses, thick with unbridled decay, lay about it as far as my eyes could see. Here death was feeding off the dead. This was the Garden of Chaos. Vile creatures nested amongst the bones of the dead, there to gnaw at the fallen and fill the air with sickly sounds of merriment.

Here dark trees had petrified, their shapes indescribable and their essence corrupt. The graves of the fallen had become a rich loam, sucked upon by the trees of that dark forest. Pierced by the tree roots, the dead had stirred once more and each branch bore a skull, mildewed and heavy with loathing.

In that place I looked upon the fate of mankind and wept for the future.'

- *Liber Malefic*

THE DAEMONS OF NURGLE

Nurgle's daemon legions march out to the dolorous tolling of rusted bells. They trudge, caper and squirm beneath roaring storm clouds of flies. Wherever they go the land sickens and rots, bastions of order collapsing into mouldering rubble in order to make way for the festering dominion of Nurgle.

Each of the Ruinous Powers has armies of daemons at their command. Formed from the energies of the deities themselves, these beings are extensions of their god's will. Everything about them echoes the divine entity that created them, from their physical aspect and ways of war, to their motivations and desires. The daemons of Chaos are every bit their master's creatures, and though they exhibit personalities and agendas of their own, their every thought and deed is driven by the essential nature of the god that created them.

The daemons of Nurgle are plague-infested abominations, beings of sanity-blasting foulness whose stench alone is enough to stun a bull demi-gryph. They exist solely to spread the myriad contagions of their master to every corner of reality and beyond, a goal they pursue with single-minded determination. Their mere presence is enough to spark epidemics that devastate nations, and when they march to battle together they are entropy and the misery of terminal sickness given physical form.

Yet for all their repugnance, the daemons of Nurgle are – by and large – neither as hateful nor as cruel as the other daemons of Chaos. Just as the most virulent malady kills without malice or distinction, so too do Nurgle's daemons. They march to battle with a mixture of morose detachment and obscene good cheer, and the slaughter that they wreak amongst their foes is but a by-product of their desire to infect all with the dubious blessings of their magnanimous god.

Great Unclean Ones lead the parade, lumbering mountains of rancid flesh and seeping pustules crowned with splintered antlers of rotting bone. Echoes of their master, these greater daemons are monstrous and ebullient in equal measure, chortling at the antics of their lesser kin or singing in gurgling baritones even as they spew infectious filth across their enemies.

Plaguebearers make up the shambling masses of Nurgle's daemon legions.

EPIDEMIUS

Epidemius is Nurgle's chosen Tallyman, one of the seven Proctors of Pestilence and the cataloguer of all the Plague God's diseases. Epidemius' task is an unending one, and it requires a great deal of record keeping, so he rides a creaking wooden palanquin to allow him to focus on his duties and to more easily force a path through Nurgle's hordes. This mouldering litter is borne aloft by a rolling mound of Nurglings, who assist their master by operating the death's head abacus incorporated into its frame. From his perch, Epidemius surveys the thrift and splendour of the Plague God's creations, making note of mortality and infection rates with the aid of his hourglass, as well as secondary symptoms such as unusual discolouration, curiously shaped growths and novel odours.

As Epidemius' tally rises ever higher, Nurgle looks down with fatherly pride, bestowing his godly gifts upon the Tallyman and his servants. Thus, in performing his allotted duties, Epidemius acts as a locus of infectious might for the daemons fighting around him. Nurgle's favour renders his daemons stronger, more poisonous and more resilient, which in turn enables them to spread his plagues all the quicker.

Epidemius has travelled the Mortal Realms since before the Age of Chaos began, and his meandering course follows no discernable pattern. Yet always he arrives in time to record each of Nurgle's proudest outbreaks, his brow furrowed in concentration as he studies the hideous demise of another army foolish enough to reject Nurgle's beneficence.

They are one-eyed grotesques whose distended bodies are home to myriad diseases, and they clutch dripping plague swords in their withered claws as they trudge toward the foe. The Plaguebearers are led by Heralds of Nurgle, from the sorcerous Poxbringers and spiteful Spoilpox Scriveners, to the capering Sloppity Bilepipers who whirl clumsily through the ranks, cracking revolting jokes and playing discordant tunes upon their rasping gutpipes.

Plague Drones thrum overhead, Plaguebearers mounted upon enormous Rot Flies that hurl pus-filled death's heads into the enemy ranks. Beasts of Nurgle bound across the battlefield, each one a crushing mass of slime-slick muscle and lashing tentacles whose only desire is to hurl itself into the fray in search of living playthings.

Wherever the daemon legions of Nurgle march, a living carpet of Nurglings swarms towards the foe. Diminutive and mischievous, these jabbering mites fill the air with a gabbling cacophony barely less disturbing than their indescribable reek, and pour over the enemy lines in a biting, scratching tide.

For all the nauseating spectacle of their advance, one could be mistaken for believing Nurgle's daemons to be less warlike than their counterparts. At first glance, they might seem plodding and cumbersome by comparison. Yet Nurgle's children are every bit as dangerous as their rivals, just in very different ways.

The greatest strength of these abhorrent entities is their extraordinary resilience to damage. Volleys of arrows and hails of bullets rebound from their leathery hides, or simply lodge in layers of fat to little effect. Sword thrusts punch through rotted organs and muscle without causing the daemons any discomfort at all. Worse, as assailants try desperately to wrench their weapons free of the creatures' blubber, they are showered with a deadly cocktail of diseased and corrosive bodily fluids.

'What repulsive beauty I see before me! Such noxious purity! Such nauseating hope! No, no, no, by Nurgle's roilbloated guts, this ghastly land must feel the touch of rot!'

- *Lord Moulgh Blacknail during the invasion of Shimmerdell*

Even spellcraft, artillery fire or the talons of monstrous beasts can be confounded by the unholy resilience of Nurgle's daemons. All the while, they advance inexorably upon their panicked enemies, before unleashing their own hideous weapons of war. These, unfortunately for all the denizens of the Mortal Realms, are manifold and truly repulsive.

Some daemons wield plagueswords, weapons that drip with contagions so lethally infectious that a single nick or cut spells an agonising death. Others can vomit jetting floods of viscous bile to drown their enemies or else leave them mired in a sucking morass of lethal pestilence. Lashing tentacles, rotting fangs and filth-smeared claws batter and tear at the enemy, while paralytic mucus renders them helpless before the sorcerous contagions that billow around the daemons in choking clouds.

Blinded by swarms of flies, deafened by the dull clangour of bells and gongs, choked by the putrid stench that thickens the air, many foes feel their sanity or courage reach breaking point. They turn to flee, screaming in revulsion and horror. Most are so riddled with disease that they will not get far, while those who do serve only to spread a bow wave of plague and sickness before the daemons' advance.

Even should an enemy stand their ground, and succeed in striking down one of Nurgle's daemons, the creature will not truly be slain. Instead, with its mortal shell torn asunder, the essence of the daemon is banished back to the Garden of Nurgle. There it must languish amidst fetor and filth, nothing more than an echo of its true power.

Eventually the cycles of rot and rebirth that sweep through Nurgle's garden will see a banished entity recorporealise, though each sort of daemon that serves the Plague God is reborn in its own strange and horrible fashion. Some develop within quivering pupae that dangle amongst the sagging foliage of steaming swamps, while others manifest as embryonic growths suspended within the yolk-like pus of cysts that appear upon the hides of larger daemons. The only constant regarding these resurrections is how unutterably disgusting they are to those who do not share Nurgle's particular eye for beauty.

AVATARS OF CORRUPTION

Many and varied are the wars waged by the daemons of Nurgle. From the mind-bending hellscapes of the Realm of Chaos, to the corporeal battlefields of the Mortal Realms, Nurgle's daemon legions are hurled or summoned into battle on sevenfold new fronts every hour.

The Realm of Chaos is an abomination beyond the imaginings of mortals. The armies of the Dark Gods march across splinters of sundered reality. They fight over endless fields of skulls that sprawl in the shadow of titanic metal volcanoes. They make war through multifaceted crystalline labyrinths in which every thought and deed sends a thousand shattered reflections cascading into madness. They clash in foetid jungles where the plants are formed from soul-stuff and squirming insects, and across landscapes of rippling flesh that split open to devour combatants or discharge geysers of perfumed ichor that rain down as glittering jewels. Amidst such riotous insanity, even the hardiest mortal armies would not long survive. Thus it is that Nurgle sends his daemon legions – the Plague Legions – to fight his battles against his brother gods.

When battling in the Realm of Chaos, Nurgle's armies are notable for their stolid organisation and relentlessness. For all their eccentricities, the Great Unclean Ones that lead the Plague Legions to war are highly intelligent beings who understand well the cut and thrust of war. They view the enemy's forces like a disease might view a crowd of potential victims, were it possessed of malign intent. The foe must be worn down by increments, gradually lumbered with ever greater corruptions until they perish under the unbearable weight of their afflictions. Meanwhile, the enemy's every effort to halt the Plague Legions' advance or drive them back must be resisted, lest the foe cure themselves of the infection.

Through fell magics, the lords of Nurgle's legions cloud the air with poisonous miasmas and roaring fly-storms to conceal their warriors. They summon vast constructs fashioned from chaotic energies, snail-like monstrosities the size of mountains with pox-ridden castles lurching upon their backs, or else flood the field with diseased slime, the better to mire the daemons of rival gods.

So are Nurgle's battles in the Realm of Chaos fought, whether he is invading his brothers' domains or defending the tumbledown walls of his garden. Battle in the Mortal Realms, however, is a rather more anarchic affair. Corrupted Realmgates do lead from the Garden of Nurgle into other realms, and during especially fearsome conflicts entire Plague Legions trudge from the depths of these portals. However, the number of such Realmgates has been thinned by the determined efforts of Sigmar's Stormcast Eternals. Some

HORTICULOUS SLIMUX

There are those who say that Horticulous Slimux was the very first Plaguebearer created by Nurgle. Certainly, he has been the custodian of Nurgle's garden for as long as even the most ancient Great Unclean Ones can recall.

Gnarled and leathery like a rotted apple left too long in the sun, Horticulous is a pragmatic and humourless being with a no-nonsense approach to battle and gardening alike. Sitting astride his lumbering molluscoid steed – known affectionately to Horticulous as Mulch – the Gardener ploughs ever onward through Nurgle's domains, tilling the foetid soil with his Gruntleplough and casting an experienced eye over the festering flora all around him.

Horticulous prefers the familiar surrounds of the Garden of Nurgle to the comparative sterility of the Mortal Realms. When compelled by Nurgle to lead his Plague Legions to war, the Gardener is thus sour and bad tempered, despising the cleanliness of the realms and blaming their denizens for every pang of worry he feels about his temporarily untended meadows. In battle, Horticulous conjures the power of Nurgle's garden and ushers it into reality, overrunning sites of sorcerous power with its boundless fecundity. He is accompanied by romping packs of Beasts of Nurgle, whose foolishness he always forgives, and who look to him like hounds do their master. Though he might seem slow, Horticulous is relentless, and champions beyond count have fallen to the rusty snick of his pruning blades.

have been cleansed while others – the most hopelessly infested – have been destroyed altogether, denying Nurgle's armies of their use.

In many regions of the Mortal Realms, the daemons of Nurgle must find more esoteric means by which to launch their assaults. The most common of these are the summoning rituals of Nurgle's many mortal worshippers, which must be performed where reality has become most horribly corrupted and the foul Filth Pits have been dug. Where misery and disease are rife, there sprout burgeoning groves of Rotwoods, Bulgebarks, Feculent Gnarlmaws and other disgusting flora. These bell-hung trees thrust their roots deep into the Realm of Chaos, forming conduits by which the Plague God's daemons may cross into reality.

The summoning of daemons is no simple matter – great reserves of dark magic are required, and the necessary rites must be meticulously observed lest the prospective summoner risk their soul becoming a plaything for the very beings they sought to call upon. When the rituals are performed correctly, however, the veil is torn and the daemons of Nurgle spill forth.

Such passages into the Mortal Realms do not last long, and unless a specific legion or daemon is summoned through the use of its True Name, the entities that emerge are whichever daemons of Nurgle were fortunate enough to squirm their way through

from the Realm of Chaos. Sometimes this will be a single Tallyband, plucked from the midst of battle. At others it is a random agglomeration of daemons, snatched up from the Garden of Nurgle and deposited suddenly in the Mortal Realms. Whatever the case, the daemons soon forge a rough and ready hierarchy amongst themselves, for they are much more interested in this new opportunity to spread contagion and misery in the name of their god than in bickering over protocol.

Especially virulent outbreaks of plague can also thin the veil enough to coax Nurgle's daemons into the Mortal Realms. Such names as the City of Mists, Gallowhaven and the Morientae Reach are whispered with dread by those who know their sorry tales, of the hideous outbreaks that tore through their populations, and of the subsequent invasion by the daemonic legions of Nurgle.

So fell the Pristine Heart in Ghyran during the earliest days of the War of Life, and so too was the city of Astralon turned from glory to horror. That magnificent city – built around the Gildenglass Realmgate following its capture by the Astral Templars – saw its first case of Nodding Bloat precisely seven years to the day after its foundation stones were laid. Brought into the city by refugees from the Tusked Hills, the disease spread like wildfire through Astralon's streets. The cramped alleyways of the inner districts were soon choked with ruptured corpses and seething carpets of vermin. When the epidemic reached its height the Plague Legions burst into the city's overburdened healing halls. The war between Astralon's defenders and Nurgle's daemons has raged ever since, and shows no signs of remission.

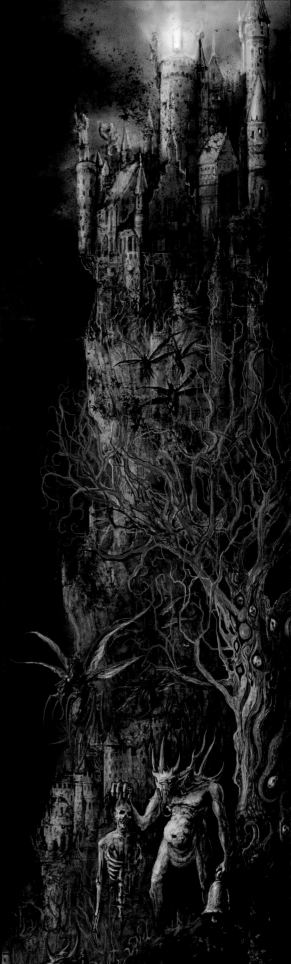

ROTBRINGERS

Vast mortal armies are pledged to the service of Nurgle, countless hordes fighting and dying for the Plague God throughout the Mortal Realms. The greatest of these are chosen by Nurgle as his favourites, and blessed with his virulent boons.

There are many reasons why the denizens of the Mortal Realms turn to the worship of Nurgle. Since the Age of Chaos began, myriad epidemics have swept across the lands. Believing themselves abandoned by the gods they once worshipped and scorning the ineffectual ministrations of their healers, many mortals have offered desperate prayers to Nurgle. The Plague God has alleviated the suffering of such unfortunates – if not their symptoms – but only at the cost of their souls, and of their eternal service to him.

Others, seeing their homes and lands despoiled, have given in to despair. Nurgle welcomes all such wretches, teaching them first to appreciate, then to cherish the entropy and rot that surrounds them, and to spread it far and wide as the gift it truly is.

The twisted and disfigured, the spiteful and forsaken, the hopelessly insane; all embrace the paternal comfort offered by Grandfather Nurgle, and willingly draw strength from the foul blessings that he rains down upon them.

Not all who enter Nurgle's service do so intentionally. In his own chortling fashion, Nurgle is the master of manipulating good intentions to gruesome ends. Many are the physicians, alchemists and holy men who seek to better understand the nature of disease, hoping to halt the spread of plague. Nurgle is only too happy to offer his forbidden secrets to such individuals, tempting them ever further down paths of bitter revelation until their good intentions curdle along with their souls. All this has led tribes,

cities, even entire nations to turn to the worship of Nurgle. Throughout the Mortal Realms, immense armies of flyblown warriors march into battle, crying out praise to the Plague God.

Dreadholds are captured in Nurgle's name, their walls slick with ooze, their battlements shot through with sentient corrosion. Slinking plague-cults infiltrate the Cities of Sigmar, gathering in deep sewer chambers to perform unclean rites and taint waterways with virulent filth. Pestilential Brayherds haunt trackless forests, despoiling all that is green and good. Enclaves of civilisation are torn down or corrupted from within. Vast and noble beasts are brought low by the weapons of sickness and entropy. All of these terrible deeds are intended to please Nurgle and thus earn his favour. Those who are chosen will be elevated to the ranks of the Rotbringers.

Some warriors of Nurgle are blessed simply for laying a mighty hero low in battle, or driving Nurgle's enemies from the field in disarray. This is rare, however, for simple martial conquest is a little crude for Nurgle's tastes. Rather than see another god's champion slain, he would prefer they were infected with some strain of his poxes, so that their only hope is to forsake whichever of Nurgle's brothers they worship and give their allegiance to him instead. More than just defeating an enemy army in battle, Nurgle prefers to see its soldiers infected with choice contagions, and enough of their number left alive that – in their panicked flight – they taint their allies' strongholds, and spread his gifts to all those they encounter.

Amongst the ranks of the Rotbringers are those who have poisoned the rations of their former comrades with plague spores, infected the drinking water of island-borne fortresses, and raised statues of soiled warpstone the better to reduce places of magical beauty to bubbling slime.

However they earned their blessings, and no matter how starved or gnarled in stature they were before Nurgle marked them, most Rotbringers are hulking giants. Their massive frames are so swollen with rancid flab and layered muscle that in many places their skin splits open, allowing putrid organs to spill forth.

'Oh great Nurgle, accept this offering of blood and filth! Witness my devotion and send your might to slither through my clotted veins! With this sacrifice I beseech thee!'

- Hulghor Hexenrott, upon striking down Nestyria the Pure

What armour they wear is often buckled and rent from the pressure exerted by their distended forms, and any metal protection is invariably thick with rust or verdigris. This matters

little, for Rotbringers boast an unholy resilience. They know nothing of pain, and – between their leathery hides and the fact that in many cases their bodies heal damage as quickly as it can be inflicted – only the most dolorous blow will do enough damage to slow them down, let alone slay them.

In return, the Rotbringers hew their way through their enemies like harvestmen in reaping season. Their massive frames house unnatural might sufficient to hack an armoured knight in two with a single swing. Even those enemies who evade the rusted axes and rattling flails that the Rotbringers wield soon find themselves succumbing to the aura of plague that surrounds them.

Buzzing storms of flies blanket the battlefield when the Rotbringers march to war, crawling frantically into eyes, noses and screaming mouths. Parasitic horrors bite and sting, and every breath the foe takes draws daemon spores and spoiled air into their lungs, until their flesh breaks out in angry buboes and pus weeps from every pore.

Some Rotbringers are gifted with rusting tocsins that erode the enemy's will to fight with every toll, or items so saturated with unwholesome magic that they can set loose Nurgle's diseases amongst the enemy's ranks with but a simple word or gesture. Others ride cadaverous steeds that fill the hearts of their foes with dread, or else are borne into battle atop grotesque daemonic fly-beasts. However they go to war, and whatever baleful weapons they wield, all Rotbringers are terrifyingly powerful warriors, high in their god's favour.

WORSHIP THROUGH DESECRATION

The Rotbringers are fervently devoted to their beloved Grandfather Nurgle. They are thankful for his generosity and protective of his foul creations, reserving their wrath for the ungrateful worshippers of other gods who – they believe – must be shown the error of their ways, even if it kills them.

From Putrid Blightkings to Maggoth Riders, Pusgoyle Blightlords to the mighty Glottkin themselves, the Rotbringers exhibit a gallows humour and a joy in their work, stemming from an acceptance that, inevitably, all must rot and perish. This malignant mirth is entirely at odds with the way in which they make war, showing neither mercy nor forgiveness to those who would oppose Grandfather Nurgle.

The Rotbringers crush the armies of Order wherever they encounter them, despoiling everything their foes hold dear. They hew through the warbands of Nurgle's brother gods, spreading the blessings of disease and decay as widely as they can in the hopes of securing converts from amongst the enemy ranks. Where they encounter temples and shrines to other deities, they desecrate them with muck and mire,

making examples of any attendant priests and holy men to cow the flocks of unfaithful.

Nurgle's mortal armies go to especial pains to taint sites of life-giving power, such as sky-falls, springs and realmstone deposits, for to successfully imbue such places with Nurgle's gifts is to spread them far and wide using the natural cycles of life. To further propagate their god's corruptions, the Rotbringers excavate vast earthworks known as Filth Pits that are bored using chained wyrr-maggots. These deep holes look, from above, like the sigil of Nurgle writ large in leprous craters. Their sides are sheer and slippery with unspeakable substances, while their depths sit several feet deep in a parasite-infested gruel that bubbles and pops as it gives off clouds of airborne contagions.

Not only do Filth Pits poison the land for miles around, but they are also used by the Rotbringers as sacrificial sites. Captive warriors are flung into their depths, there to suffer one horrible pox and infestation after another until at last they perish in miserable agony. Such drawn-out suffering offers great praise to Nurgle, and gradually wears thin the weave of reality, creating weak points through which the Plague God's daemons can more easily be summoned.

Those Rotbringers who achieve truly great deeds in Nurgle's name are elevated to positions of command. Infested with voracious parasites and riddled with the most lethal diseases, they become Lords of Nurgle, and lead the Rotbringers to war. Some of these champions fight at the head of immense armies of mortal warriors, while others march to war alongside Nurgle's daemon legions, offering awed praise to the daemon lords who, for their part, view the Lords of Nurgle with paternal affection and amusement. Still other Plague Lords choose to surround themselves with small, elite bands of Rotbringers and travel the Mortal Realms on quests to bring their god's gifts to new lands.

When embarking upon especially challenging conquests or defending their mouldering fastnesses from overwhelming attack, the Rotbringers may forge alliances with other factions. Though sometimes they enslave diseased Brayherds or foully tainted monsters, more commonly the Rotbringers forge temporary pacts with the skaven of the Clans Pestilens.

Though ultimately Nurgle and the Horned Rat seek different ends for the Mortal Realms, the followers of both deities employ disease and despair as weapons of war, and so fight well together upon the field of battle. Often the Rotbringers will allow their ratmen allies to surge ahead in a chittering horde, suffering the brunt of the enemy's wrath and overrunning their lines before Putrid Blightkings and daemons wade in to strike the killing blow. At other times, the Clans Pestilens will support Rotbringer attacks with vile magics and batteries of plague-flinging war machines. Yet always the servants of Nurgle must keep a wary eye on their opportunistic allies, for the slightest sign of weakness is enough to spur the skaven to violent acts of betrayal.

A few amongst the Rotbringers' ranks have become dark legends within the Mortal Realms. Names such as Festus the Leechlord, Gutrot Spume, the Maggoth Lords and the Glottkin are whispered with fear and hate across Ghyran and beyond. Yet Nurgle's esteem, much like his power, is cyclical. The Brothers Glott, in particular, have risen several times to the very apogee of the Plague God's regard, only to plunge out of favour again when their conquests have gone awry. At such times these Rotbringer heroes may vanish for decades, even centuries at a time, typically consigned to some inventive punishment or other by their god. Yet Nurgle can never stay angry with his most dedicated of followers for long, and always they return to win back his favour.

TORGLUG THE DESPISED

Amongst the greatest of Nurgle's mortal champions was Torglug, he who once was Tornus, champion and defender of the Lifewells. Hurled into a Filth Pit by Nurgle's conquering hordes, Tornus was so proud, and so determined not to succumb, that he endured seventy-seven days of suffering before crawling from the pit as a newly empowered Rotbringer. Taking the name Torglug, this lumbering destroyer showed his devotion to Nurgle by corrupting the very thing he once sought to protect, tainting the Ghyran Lifewells and leading a Rotbringer horde to ever greater conquests. At the last, it was Torglug who nearly seized the soulpod of the goddess Alarielle, the prize that would have ensured Nurgle's final dominion over the Realm of Life.

Yet in that moment, the Celestant-Prime struck Torglug down with Sigmar's own hammer, Ghal Maraz. Driven from his diseased body, the Plague Lord's once noble soul was hurled upwards, to Sigmar's Heavens, where it was torturously and painstakingly cleansed of Nurgle's taint. Reforged by divine lightnings, Torglug has become Tornus once more, a Knight-Venator who hunts the servants of Nurgle with a single-minded hatred. For their part, the Rotbringers now know him as Torglug the Ungrateful, Torglug the Wasteful or Torglug the Fool. Upon Nurgle's orders they seek him every bit as fervently as he seeks them. If this turncoat nemesis could be tainted again, then surely Nurgle's supremacy over Sigmar would be proven. Of course, Nurgle would not be so kindly to Tornus a second time…

ARMIES OF THE PLAGUE GOD

Endless armies of daemons and mortals make war in Nurgle's name. From small warbands to nation-toppling hordes, from mortal war parties to trudging legions from the Dark God's own garden, these armies blight the lands and desecrate all before them in their efforts to bring rot and ruin.

PLAGUE LEGIONS

Nurgle's daemon armies are known as Plague Legions. It is said that there are as many Plague Legions as there are spores floating through the miasmal air of the Garden of Nurgle and, while they might be individually somewhat smaller than their counterparts in the ranks of the other Dark Gods, their numbers more make up for this. Each Plague Legion is led by a Great Unclean One, whose personal eccentricities influence its composition and tactics. Some Great Unclean Ones favour airborne armadas of Plague Drones,

while others enjoy burying the foe beneath slobbering packs of Beasts of Nurgle, or slowly grinding them down with waves of grumbling Plaguebearers. Beneath the Great Unclean One stand his lieutenants, who can be Heralds or subordinate greater daemons. Though technically known as the Rancid Retinue, these lesser commanders are collectively bestowed with grandiloquent titles of their leader's invention, such as Lords of Fulsome Filth, the Decayed Hands of Almighty Foulness, or the Bubotic Masters of Slopsome Generosity.

The bulk of a Plague Legion is composed of seven Tallybands. Each of these comprises seven packs of Plaguebearers and Plague Drones, led by a Herald of Nurgle. These are accompanied by Nurgle's most rambunctious daemons, the Beasts of Nurgle and Nurglings. So anarchic are these creatures that they stand outside the organisation of the Plague Legions, and are rarely factored directly into the Great Unclean Ones' battleplans. They spill into battle alongside their more regimented kin, adding their own enthusiastic contributions to the battle.

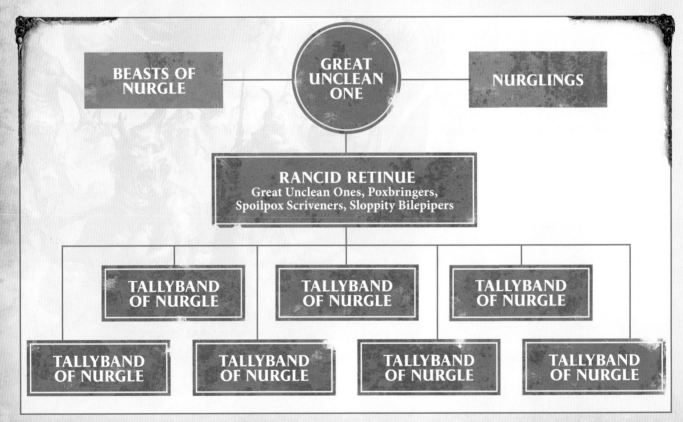

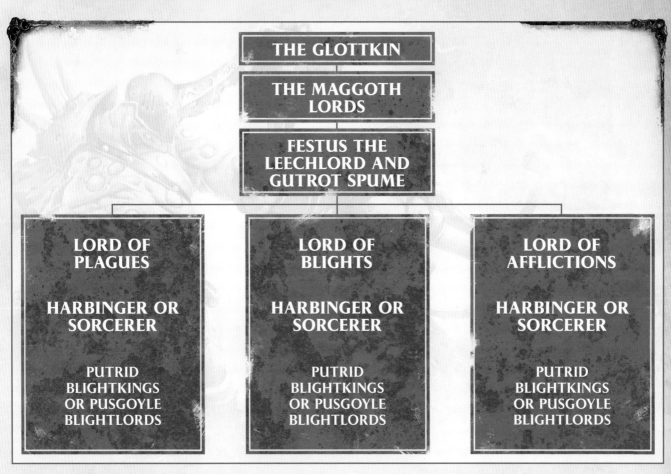

| THE GLOTTKIN |
| THE MAGGOTH LORDS |
| FESTUS THE LEECHLORD AND GUTROT SPUME |

LORD OF PLAGUES	LORD OF BLIGHTS	LORD OF AFFLICTIONS
HARBINGER OR SORCERER	HARBINGER OR SORCERER	HARBINGER OR SORCERER
PUTRID BLIGHTKINGS OR PUSGOYLE BLIGHTLORDS	PUTRID BLIGHTKINGS OR PUSGOYLE BLIGHTLORDS	PUTRID BLIGHTKINGS OR PUSGOYLE BLIGHTLORDS

ROTBRINGER CONTAGIUMS

The conquering armies of the Rotbringers are known as Contagiums. The number of Contagiums that beset the Mortal Realms varies wildly, their ranks swelling to epidemic proportions at times, and withering away to dregs at others. Typically, a Contagium is built around three warbands known as Cysts. Each Cyst comprises multiple bands of Putrid Blightkings and Pusgoyle Blightlords, and is directed in battle by a champion of the Plague God. Though there are exceptions, most Contagiums include a Cyst led by a Lord of Plagues, one led by a Lord of Blights, and one ruled over by a Lord of Afflictions, for the Rotbringers believe such is

the sacred trinity of Nurgle. These lords are advised by Sorcerers, or else accompanied by the ominous figure of a Harbinger of Decay.

The three lords establish a hierarchy amongst themselves, either through brute force, treachery or feats of endurance, so that in battle all the warriors of a Contagium know who holds authority in a given situation.

That is not to say that these warriors are not in constant competition, nor that they are locked in an endless struggle to hold the greater portion of Nurgle's favour. It is simply that, as with the powers of the Plague God himself, there is a natural order to decay and rebirth that all must obey.

Above the Cysts of each Contagium stand Nurgle's greatest champions. Such individuals as the Maggoth Lords, Gutrot Spume or the Glottkin are renowned throughout the Rotbringer ranks, and should such a favoured warrior appear in order to assume command, they will do so with little effort, for all know them as the arbiters of Nurgle's will.

WARBANDS OF THE PLAGUE GOD

The Munificent Wanderers are one of Nurgle's most prolific Plague Legions. They are led by the notoriously generous Great Unclean One Thrombolhox the Giving. These daemons diligently ensure their physical forms are infested with the greatest possible volume of Nurgle's foul gifts before striking out into the Mortal Realms. There they spread Nurgle's blessings far and wide, so that none are left wanting.

The symbol of the tri-bell echoes the Wanderers' generous call for all to come and partake of Nurgle's gifts.

The Befouling Host's sigil is the rusting star, a trio of plagueswords infested with vile spores.

Notable for their distinctive pallid flesh, the Befouling Host patrol the quinsic glades of Nurgle's garden and garrison the thorned hedge-forts around its borders. When they march out to war, they are led by the Great Unclean One Bul'gla'throx, and often accompanied by Horticulous Slimux himself. They have a fondness for infecting their victims with parasitic plague spores that transform their hosts into living fungus-nurseries.

The Droning Guard are a Plague Legion that excels in airborne attack, known throughout the Sallowlands and beyond. From the vast clouds of flies belched by their Great Unclean One, Uncle Septuklus, to the thrumming swarms of Plague Drones that form the vanguard of their assaults, this legion chokes the skies with winged horrors. Wherever their daemons tread, a stifling miasma clots the air, bringing foes to their knees.

The plague fly is a badge of great honour, bestowed on Septuklus as a reward from Nurgle himself.

The Blessed Sons are not a single Contagium, but an elite brotherhood of many. Their armour is rotten green in hue, a mark of devotion to Grandfather Nurgle, and they have fought across great swathes of Ghyran, Aqshy and Ghur beside such heroes as the Maggoth Lords and the Glottkin. Between their many Cysts, the Blessed Sons number hundreds of thousands of warriors, all swollen with pride at their revolting achievements.

The Blessed Sons use the mark of the chitinous triptych, said to hold the three secrets of endless rotting.

The icon of the Drowned Men is a corroded trident set over a tri-lobe, in honour of their piratical lord.

Clad in verdigrised copper, their bloated flesh seeping brine, the Drowned Men are well named. This is the Contagium that follows Gutrot Spume to war, their Cysts broken up into warbands who sail over water, land and air alike in rotting and sorcerously infested hulks. The Drowned Men specialise in raiding tactics, striking from unexpected quarters and sowing as much disease and destruction as possible before making their escape.

The Filthbringers are rightly feared for the dark magics and foul poisons they employ in battle. Clad in reeking maggotbone armour, these twisted warriors are led by covens of Nurgle Sorcerers, whose spellcraft spreads plague amongst the enemy and summons daemons to support their Cysts. Often seen in the company of Festus the Leechlord, this Contagium is infamous for snatching up hapless foes to test their latest concoctions upon.

The Filthbringers' three-horned skull symbol is greatly feared as a signifier of unnatural and incurable disease.

ANNALS OF ENTROPY

Since the Age of Myth, Nurgle has waged his revolting wars throughout the realms of gods and mortals alike. Though his power waxes and wanes, always his armies rise again to crush the enemy beneath their trudging advance.

THE AGE OF CHAOS

Nurgle's armies surged across the realms. The War of Life turned ever in his favour, while in Shyish he punished those who would pervert the cycle of death and decay for their selfish ends.

GESTATION AND GENESIS

With Alarielle's rebirth, the War of Life turned against Nurgle. Even the Glottkin could not stop the Everqueen from closing the Genesis Gate, the Eightpoints' link to Ghyran. Angry and despondent, the Plague God fell into a fugue that robbed his followers of power, spreading like an epidemic of misery through their ranks and leading to one defeat after another.

THE DROWNED MOUNTAIN

The duardin kingdom of Kazar-Mout thought themselves safe in their volcano-maw fortress. Yet with the coming of Rotigus, the volcano's fires were doused and its lava turned to seething pus from which seven thousand daemons crawled.

AN UNHOLY QUEST

Disgraced in defeat, the Glottkin set themselves a mighty task to win back Nurgle's favour. Gathering huge armies, they vowed to spread seven hundred and seventy seven plagues across the Mortal Realms.

BREAKING NEW GROUND

Nurgle charged Horticulous Slimux with a new task. The Gardener set out, roaming the Mortal Realms in search of sites of sorcerous fecundity. At each, he sowed seeds of contagion that grew quickly and brought the Garden of Nurgle surging into reality. Ancient wonders and mighty strongholds alike were buried in fecund foulness, but still Horticulous kept planting.

AIRBORNE CONTAGION

The Skyrealm of Ghur came entirely under the rule of Lord Asphyxos Sporelung, a mighty champion of the Rotbringers. Armadas of fly-riding killers fell upon the kingdoms below, descending amidst miasmal plague clouds.

FROM THE FILTH BELOW

Festus the Leechlord began his foul works in the sewers beneath the city of Templarum. Plagues ravaged the city's populace, before an army of Rotbringers and monks of the Clans Pestilens rose up to sacrifice the survivors to Nurgle. Festus claimed the befouled city, renaming it the Leech's Lair.

THE PANDAEMONIC WARS

Foreseeing Nurgle's resurgence and wishing to prevent it, Tzeentch invaded the Garden of Nurgle. Prismatic spears as tall as mountains rained down, armies of sorcerous daemons streaming from within them. Nurgle's legions counter-attacked, and the fighting spilled into the Mortal Realms in a campaign spanning several kingdoms.

THE MAGGOT PIT

Atop the Howling Plateau of the Chamon Hinterwastes, Morbidex Twiceborn and Orghotts Daemonspew led the defeat of the Bulgut Tribes. Their army dug a vast Filth Pit, hurling in the strongest ogor captives and a single maggot. A hideous feast ensued as the maggot chewed through one bellowing victim after another, multiplying again and again. From the ensuing seething mass of larvae, Bloab Rotspawned was resurrected.

THE FASTNESS BESET

An immense horde of Rotbringers, plague daemons, Slaves to Darkness and Nurgle-worshipping Brayherds advanced upon the Greywater Fastness. Knowing the power of the city's super-weapons, they began to systematically poison the lands around it with Filth Pits and Feculent Gnarlmaws. As the forces of Order counter-attacked, a churning war zone developed.

ROOT AND ROT

As the forces of Order continued their grinding advance in Ghyran, an alliance of Ironbark sylvaneth and Fyreslayer mercenaries overran the Deepenroot Vaults. They were quick to fete their victory over the Clans Pestilens. Yet the ratmens' deaths fuelled a vast summoning ritual, conjuring Rotigus Rainfather and Epidemius at the head of seven Plague Legions. The daemons of Nurgle laid siege to the horrified forces of Order, beginning a conflict that became more bitter and horrific by the day.

WRATH OF THE LAND KRAKEN

Leading an alliance of Contagiums including the Drowned Men and the Hands of Filth, Gutrot Spume attacked Hammerhal Aqsha. Though his army was driven back, they sowed sickness and death through the outer districts.

THE INSIDIOUS TAINT

Sigmar and his allies could not remain ignorant of Horticulous Slimux's mission forever, and as the Garden of Nurgle spread, so they saw the danger at last. Nurgle had warded his lieutenant well, however, and so the God-King was forced to send his most fleet-footed Rangers to track down and banish the Gardener. Led by Knight-Zephyros Neave Blacktalon, the Rangers began their hunt, determined to stop the rot.

THE DRONING

From corrupted Realmgates and infested plague-groves, storms of flies erupted to cloud the skies of the Mortal Realms. Beneath their shadow, poxes flourished, and in their wake the armies of Nurgle blackened the land. The Plague God's new war upon all the realms had begun, and his foes would know well his displeasure.

GREAT UNCLEAN ONES

The Great Unclean Ones are Nurgle's mightiest daemons. Towering over their enemies, these living hillocks of rotting flesh lumber across the battlefield swinging their rusted weapons, vomiting streams of filth and unleashing diseased magics upon the foe.

The outward appearance of the Great Unclean Ones echoes that of Nurgle himself. Their immense bodies are bloated with corruption, their necrotic flesh thick with boils and buboes. Reeking pus oozes from their exposed innards, within which gurgling daemon mites and maggots the length of a man's arm squirm and sport. Such foulness evokes the fundamental truth of Nurgle's power: while life endures, there will always be ruin and decay.

Grotesquely at odds with their foulness, Great Unclean Ones are eccentric and cheerful daemons. They are intelligent and orderly beings that display a surprising grasp of grand strategy and battlefield logistics. They are gregarious and curiously sentimental, taking real pride in the efforts of their followers both mortal and daemonic. Great Unclean Ones often refer to those who worship and serve them as their 'pretties' or 'children', chuckling indulgently at their posturing, and delightedly cheering on their efforts upon the battlefield.

For all their gallows humour, and the relish with which they go about spreading misery and plague, Great Unclean Ones are terrifying when roused to wrath. Wreathed in lethal miasmas of disease, they wade through the enemy ranks, crushing foes beneath their bulk and pulping the survivors with their enormous swords and flails.

Some toll rusted summoning bells to draw forth fresh daemons from the Realm of Chaos, while others gather their sorcerous might and unleash terrible outbreaks of magical plague. Few indeed are the foes that can stand for long against such pestilential might.

Since the beginning of the Age of Chaos, certain Great Unclean Ones have earned particular infamy, their names becoming virtual curses amongst their foes. Such abominations as Bolathrax, Pupa Grotesse and the mighty Rotigus are feared and hated for the corruption they have spread, the genocides they have overseen and the gruelling, endless wars they have fomented across the Mortal Realms.

ROTIGUS

There is one amongst Nurgle's greater daemons who journeys further than any other. He trudges through lands mortal and divine, and where he goes, repugnant life spreads about him in waves. He is Rotigus, the Plague God's most beneficent servant, and as the gelid downpour of Nurgle's Deluge patters endlessly upon his cowled head he hums a phlegmy dirge. It is Rotigus who answers the desperate prayers of those beset by drought or famine, who beseech aid from the obscure demigod they know as Rainfather, Lifefont or the Bringer of Plenty. Only when this looming abomination arrives in answer to their call and their lands squirm with his generosity do his victims realise their terrible mistake. Livestock give birth to deformed young until they carpet the land in screaming, slime-slick profusion. Flora and fauna bloat and twist with grotesque fecundity, while the deluge hammers endlessly down and the filthy waters rise.

HERALDS OF NURGLE

Amongst the ranks of Nurgle's Plaguebearers stand those with an aptitude for greater things. Such notable entities, known collectively as Heralds, wield noxious magical powers or possess strange and grotesque abilities that allow them to augment and lead Nurgle's foot soldiers upon the battlefield.

POXBRINGERS

Poxbringers project an aura of malign authority. They stand taller and broader than the Plaguebearers that surround them, their lumpen heads crowned with magnificent sets of rotting antlers. These daemons are the most common lieutenants of the Great Unclean Ones, who ensure their orders are carried out to the letter. They lead their kin into battle with gallows humour. Wielding their baleswords with prodigious strength, Poxbringers hack down the enemy's champions and sorcerers while unleashing their own unclean spells to corrupt and despoil. Nurgle himself awards the most accomplished Poxbringers with extra duties, which they discharge with solemn pride. One such individual is Wretch Gab'larr, who is tasked with studying the effects of Nurgle's plagues upon specimens never before encountered, then describing them to his master upon the porch of Nurgle's Manse.

SLOPPITY BILEPIPERS

Plaguebearers infected with Chortling Murrain fall into a comedic fever, compulsively capering and quipping. Thus are Sloppity Bilepipers created, and sent with gutpipes and marotter to amuse Nurgle's Tallybands. Their jokes and songs find little purchase amidst the glum Plaguebearers, but Nurgle's other daemons find their antics hilarious. Great Unclean Ones boom belly laughs as Nurglings shriek with mirth, and the Beasts of Nurgle flop about in excited circles, confused but desperate to join in the fun. Unfortunately for Nurgle's foes, Chortling Murrain is very infectious, and can cause mortals to laugh until their sides literally split. Yet the Bilepipers themselves are always the final victims of their disease. If it goes into remission, their knack for jesting vanishes, leaving them doomed to become the next marotter and set of gutpipes for their desperately grinning replacement.

SPOILPOX SCRIVENERS

Spoilpox Scriveners are responsible for ensuring that the Plaguebearers of their Tallyband do not shirk. They are spiteful creatures, always looking to punish their fellows, and their mood upon the battlefield is worsened by their snotty and revolting allergies to the Mortal Realms. The Scriveners know the tally of diseases that must be counted, and they record the names of those Plaguebearers that lose count using scritching quills made from the plucked tail feathers of Lords of Change. All the while, the Scriveners browbeat the daemons around them, their nasal voices booming from proboscises terminating in huge mouths that can bite a man in half. Those whose names they take down risk being punished by becoming new Sloppity Bilepipers, whose tomfoolery the Scriveners despise most of all.

PLAGUEBEARERS

The bulk of Nurgle's daemon legions are made up of rank upon rank of Plaguebearers. These glum creatures shamble towards the enemy in a rotting mass, all gangling limbs, necrotic flesh and rheumy, cyclopean eyes. Like something from a nightmare, they engulf the foe before hacking them apart.

Plaguebearers are composed from the soul-stuff of mortals who have died of Nurgle's Rot. This perfect disease runs an excruciatingly slow course, during which its victim's body bloats up and rots like that of a corpse. Enduring unspeakable agonies yet wholly unable to die, the sufferer's soul is slowly eroded until eventually they welcome the misery and malignancy of their condition. Driven mad by the Plague God's foul gift, they finally perish, only to be reborn in the Garden of Nurgle as an immortal Plaguebearer.

Plaguebearers are vile creatures whose stench alone is enough to knock a troggoth unconscious. Their skin is leathery and ridden with sores and boils. Their organs are so swollen with corpse gas that many have split-open guts, from which rancid entrails dangle like old rope. A single eye stares from each Plaguebearer's ghastly face, and a single horn juts from their forehead.

The constant drone of counting surrounds bands of Plaguebearers. It is their unending task to tally the diseases that Nurgle has inflicted upon reality, and though such an undertaking is singularly impossible, still the Plaguebearers count on and on.

Facing Plaguebearers in battle is a truly daunting prospect, for their putrid bodies can withstand all but the most grievous blows. Meanwhile, though they strike at their victims but ponderously, every Plaguebearer wields a plague sword that exudes lethal filth, meaning that a single cut from its jagged edge can kill in seconds.

NURGLE'S MALIGNANT MENAGERIE

Many weird daemonic creatures infest the Garden of Nurgle, from the drooling gastrobominus and the reedy-voiced sirenleech to the filth-sifter, marrowfly and the rare and enormous behemuck. The most common of these creatures often accompany the Plague Legions to battle.

BEASTS OF NURGLE

Beasts of Nurgle are slug-like monstrosities whose enormous bodies are weighed down with slime-slick muscle and blubber. Fanged maws yawn wide in their flesh, dripping with diseased mucus, and around their heads wave clusters of pox-riddled tentacles that can throttle a man, or bite out his jugular with their lamprey fangs. An unspeakable reek wafts from the beasts' foul bodies, and paralytic goo seeps from their skin to leave trails wherever they go.

For all their horrifying aspect, the Beasts of Nurgle are enthusiastic and friendly creatures. Their simple minds know nothing of malice or spite, and as they squirm into battle they do not seek to slaughter the enemy, but to play with them. Beasts of Nurgle are always desperate for attention, and they hunt down new playmates with rambunctious glee.

Of course, the beasts' friendly disposition is of little help to enemy warriors crushed beneath their enormous bulk, or struck down by the myriad plagues that pulse from their bodies. The beasts have no idea of their own strength, hitting the enemy lines like living battering rams to crush and rend all around them as they flail with joy. Only when their playmates stop moving altogether do the beasts pause for a moment, burbling anxiously as they cast about for suddenly absent friends. Yet soon enough their beady eyes fasten on some new victim and, with delirious hoots, the Beasts of Nurgle are off once more. In their wake, the crushed remains of their last playmates bubble and pop as they slowly dissolve.

NURGLINGS

Wherever the armies of Nurgle march, they are accompanied by gabbling swarms of daemon mites known as Nurglings. Hatched from pustules within the innards of the Great Unclean Ones, these horrible little creatures infest the guts of the larger daemons, gnawing on loose flaps of flesh and lapping up seepage.

In appearance, these mischievous creatures are tiny facsimiles of Papa Nurgle, rotund and rotten, with wide, fang-filled grins, jagged little antlers, and noisome fluids squirting from every orifice. The Nurglings also ape their master's jollity, cackling and squealing as they spill across the battlefield in an undulating tide.

Even a single Nurgling has the potential to be dangerous, for their needle-sharp fangs and splintered claws crawl with disease. In large numbers they can prove lethal, for they fearlessly hurl themselves at far larger foes and bury them in a heaving mass of diseased flesh. Such an ignominious end has claimed a surprising number of mighty warriors, and in sufficient quantities Nurgling swarms can even drag down monstrous beasts such as Carnosaurs or celestial Stardrakes, biting, clawing and squishing the life out of their victims.

PLAGUE DRONES

Plague Drones are airborne daemonic cavalry, high-ranking Plaguebearers riding into battle astride enormous Rot Flies. These haughty daemons wield plague swords dipped seven times in cauldrons of Nurgle's Rot, and carry sacks of death's heads tied to their saddles. Fashioned from the stitched and wax-sealed heads of powerful mortal warriors, each death's head is full to bursting with virulent slop. When hurled into the enemy, the rotted craniums burst, spraying infectious matter across the foe.

Whilst the Plague Drones themselves are horrifying, the Rot Flies they ride into battle are worse. Should a Beast of Nurgle be rebuffed by its mortal playmates too many times, a canker of resentment germinates within it. When the beast is finally banished back to the Realm of Chaos, it flops down in the swampy filth of Nurgle's garden with a sigh of resignation. Fat flies swarm upon the beast and form a living cocoon within which something new and awful pupates. When the cocoon bursts open, a Rot Fly crawls from it fully formed, burning with spite towards all the enemies that rejected the attentions of its former incarnation.

The thrum of the flies' monstrous wings, the grotesque twitch of their dangling legs and the pulsating foulness of their bloated bodies all evoke atavistic horror in Nurgle's enemies. Yet this is as nothing to the terror they unleash when they attack. Their iron-hard stingers punch through armour, while their serrated chitin forelimbs rend flesh and break bones. Worse, their mouthparts and prehensile proboscises can stretch to swallow a victim whole, gulping down those who banished the daemon in the past and trapping them in its distended abdomen to suffer for evermore.

PLAGUESWORDS

From the least important bubo-licker to the most vaunted herald of disaster, every one of Nurgle's Tallymen has a plaguesword to call their own. Forged of ancient iron, badly rusted and festering with a thousand diseases, the slightest scratch from one of these corroded weapons can damn a mortal in an instant. Some contract the dreaded soul-blight known as Nurgle's Rot, while others are laid low by the Noxious Squirm, the Sevenfold Sloughing or any one of a billion-and-more other diseases. Such is the unnatural virulence of these contagions that they can even cause supernatural creatures to wither and fade, felling Dryads like blighted trees and eating away the ethereal essence of ghosts and ghasts until their despairing wails fade to nothingness. Plaguebearers take a dutiful pride in their plagueswords, ensuring they are always smeared in crusted layers of contagious filth, and fastidiously dulling their edges on slime-coated rocks.

THE GLOTTKIN

Few mortals have risen as high in Nurgle's regard as the Glottkin. These foul brothers have rampaged across the Mortal Realms for centuries, leaving a trail of despoilment and horror in their wake. First amongst the Rotbringers, they rule the Plague God's mortal armies with a rusted iron fist.

Many tales are told of the Glottkin, but the truth of their past is shrouded in legend. Once, it is said, they were the Brothers Glott, rare triplets born under a number of ill omens. It was as if they were marked for Nurgle, fated to serve the Plague God for eternity. If the rumours are true, the Glottkin can trace their origins back to the world-that-was.

As some of Nurgle's most favoured champions, the Glottkin have been blessed with dark gifts in abundance. Whether they were granted daemonic immortality or are unnaturally sustained by their patron is unknown, but the Glottkin's history of causing mayhem and spreading plague across the Mortal Realms is recorded in the annals of many fallen empires.

Otto Glott is the most senior of the triplets – a fact he often points out – by the merest of moments. Otto is a lordly warrior, capable of cutting down any mortal hero without so much as breaking stride. In battle, he wields a scythe anointed with the poisonous filth of his own body, swinging the weapon with such strength that it can slice a Stormcast in two. Otto's wilful optimism is all the more ghastly in one so revoltingly damned. He often whistles a harvestman's tune as he goes about his bloody work, and his leprous body is seemingly immune to pain.

Ethrac Glott is a sorcerer of Nurgle, blessed with arcane powers and an encyclopaedic knowledge of infectious disease. He is mean-spirited and cunning, with a mind that tends towards devious and elaborate plots. Like the diseases he so loves, Ethrac ebbs and flows – for periods he is manic with energy and prone to fits of fever dreams. At other times, he falls into melancholy, growing ever more insular and paranoid about imagined conspiracies.

The last of the brothers is Ghurk. As the rumours tell it, he was once the slightest of his brethren and the fairest to look upon – but no longer. So swollen has Ghurk grown that he could flatten a gargant. He possesses strength enough to uproot trees, barge down castle gates and throttle monsters with his huge tentacular arm. Meanwhile, his prodigious size allows him to carry his siblings upon his back, for the horns that grow there act as a kind of howdah. He is all but unstoppable, and can wade through storms of fire and sorcery without slowing, resolutely refusing to die no matter what violence is inflicted upon him. Yet these boons of Nurgle have come at a cost, for Ghurk is always hungry, and his mind has shrivelled, making him little more than a burbling idiot. Ghurk goes where his brothers tell him, but has meagre will of his own.

Although the two elder Glottkin argue frequently, and even Ghurk sometimes grows tired of his brethren's orders, the trio are inseparable. They have won many crucial victories in the Plague God's name, from the Great Uncleansing and the fall of Athelwyrd, to the defeat of Neferata, the Mortarch of Blood, during the Shambling Wars.

Yet the Glottkin have failed too, on more than one occasion, for their powers wax and wane like those of their god. The penance that the brothers served after Alarielle's escape at the battle of Fellfields was prolonged, but Nurgle's displeasure was greater still after their defeat at the Genesis Gate during the final battles of the Realmgate Wars. Struck down by Alarielle, the Glottkin plunged into a filth-streaked waterfall, only to be snatched up by Nurgle and cast into a prison the nature of which even garrulous Otto will not speak.

Nurgle is not a deity given to sterile endings; the cycle of blooming and decay must continue without end. Eventually he released the Glottkin. Since being set free, the brothers have gathered the Rotbringers in numbers not seen for an age. They have begun a fresh rampage across the Mortal Realms, spreading countless diseases and causing endless suffering, all to win back the Plague God's favour.

THE MAGGOTH LORDS

There are great champions amongst the Rotbringers who, through might and misadventure both, have earned the right to ride gangle-limbed pox maggoths into battle. They travel the Mortal Realms as agents of Nurgle's will, furthering his diabolical plans with every gruesome deed.

ORGHOTTS DAEMONSPEW

Half mortal and half daemon, Orghotts Daemonspew is a warrior consumed by bitterness. Rumour has it that he was the result of an unholy union between a Great Unclean One and a mortal witch, though whether such an unlikely tryst was brought about by a dark pact or something even fouler is best not to consider. Whatever the truth, Orghotts possesses many daemonic traits, from a sham immortality to tainted blood that jets in corrosive arcs should his leathery skin be pierced. However, he is no true daemon, and it is this fact that has filled him with such bile.

Orghotts believes that true daemonhood is his destiny, and the Garden of Nurgle his home by birthright. Yet Orghotts' heritage condemns him to roam the Mortal Realms, never able to truly enter the garden of his god. He has visited this realm but once, and even then it was in a dreamlike state that proved more hell than heaven, for he could not touch, taste or smell the foetid wonder all around him. During that sojourn, Orghotts claimed his paired Rotaxes, the only objects that he was able to touch. He has wielded them ever since as a reminder of the divinity that surely awaits him.

Daemonspew rides to war astride the repulsive pox maggoth known as Whippermaw, who tolerates him due to the daemonic taint that flows through his clotted veins. The beast's lash-like tongue secretes a venom so potent it can slay an ogor in moments.

Whippermaw has borne Orghotts on an endless campaign across the Mortal Realms for hundreds of years. From the Orb Infernia to the Isles of Talbion, Agholheim to the Red Crescent, Orghotts has slaughtered and corrupted all in his path, hoping against hope that Nurgle will finally reward him with true daemonhood.

MORBIDEX TWICEBORN

The leering fiend known as Morbidex Twiceborn has ravaged the Jade Kingdoms of Ghyran for centuries. Sitting heavily astride the saddle of his pox maggoth, Tripletongue, Morbidex rides into battle at the head of a squelching tide of Nurglings.

Morbidex is the chosen champion of these malevolent mites, and his revolting appearance echoes their own. He also shares the hardiness of the Nurgle daemons, shrugging off the most heinous of wounds as he leads the teeming masses to overrun the enemy's lines.

Though Morbidex was not always the vile being he is now, he was never handsome. He was born amidst a firestorm as his village burned at the hands of raiders, and was left badly scarred by the flames. Despite, or perhaps because of his injuries, Morbidex grew to be a fierce warrior and the chieftain of his tribe. Yet he never forgave his disfigurement, which he laid at the door of Tzeentch, the master of sorcerous flames.

Eventually, Morbidex set out to find the realm of the gods, and offer his service to Tzeentch's greatest rival, Nurgle. As it was, Nurgle found him first. As

Morbidex scaled a vast cliff that, as the myths went, led to the Realm of Chaos, he was engulfed by an avalanche of Nurglings. Buried alive, Morbidex believed he would perish. Instead, he survived by gasping out answers to riddles posed by the giggling daemons suffocating him. For every correct answer, the Nurglings pushed him higher through the slimy press. Yet for each mistake, they transformed an aspect of his physical form to resemble that of their own. By the time Morbidex clawed his way to freedom, he had become the Twiceborn, champion of Nurgle, Rotbringer avatar of Nurglings and scourge upon the Mortal Realms.

BLOAB ROTSPAWNED

From afar, the sorcerer Bloab Rotspawned appears to be constantly surrounded by swarms of insects. In truth, Bloab is the Swarm, and the Swarm is Bloab. He is the Lord of Daemon-flies, and his foul might is a fearsome thing to behold.

Bloab was once a lean and powerful champion, part of a nomadic tribe that venerated Nurgle with their conquests. Yet the Plague God took exception to Bloab's sadistic habits, for the young warrior found a compulsive delight in tormenting small animals and insects. Nurgle values all life, no matter how minuscule, and he became irritated that such a promising champion was wasting his spite upon the least of foes, instead of proving Nurgle's might against real enemies.

Resolving to teach Bloab a lesson, the Plague God sent a swarm of daemon-flies into his cave one night. The grinning insects poured into Bloab's snoring mouth, packing out his body and laying thousands of eggs in his innards before emerging, bloodied and jubilant, to fly away into the night.

Bloab woke in agony as the eggs hatched, and he was eaten slowly from the inside out by masses of maggots. Reduced eventually to a fleshy sack, Bloab lived still thanks to Nurgle's blessings. His lesson taught, Nurgle yet had work for Bloab Rotspawned.

Since that day the sorcerer has laboured tirelessly to spread teeming life to barren wastes and pristine glades alike. So diligent has he proved that Nurgle rewarded him with a filth-spitting pox maggoth steed named Bilespurter. Though the Lord of Daemon-flies was slain by Tornus the Redeemed during the Realmgate Wars, whispers of his return have spread far and wide. After all, none can truly kill the swarm.

ROTBRINGER LORDS

The Contagiums of the Rotbringers are led by powerful champions of Nurgle, grotesque warriors who have perpetrated foul deeds in his name and walked far along the Path to Glory. Each pursues the ultimate prize of daemonhood, and will overcome any hardship or foe to win it.

LORDS OF AFFLICTIONS

Astride a massive Rot Fly, the Lord of Afflictions spearheads the Rotbringer charge. The wings of his revolting steed streak the sky with foulness as he leads attack waves of fly-mounted mortals and daemons directly into the heart of the enemy's forces.

A Lord of Afflictions is a plague vector supreme, whose principal duty to Nurgle is the spreading of contagions and parasites. Like an airborne phage he bypasses barricades and fortress walls, such physical obstacles powerless to hold him back as he drones ponderously overhead.

Those enemies facing a Lord of Afflictions must first contend with his dolorous tocsin, the weighty iron wrecking bell that trails beneath his steed. As his Rot Fly swoops down, the dolorous tocsin slams through the enemy ranks. Warriors are smashed from their feet by the bell's great weight, every impact sending a doleful toll rolling across the battlefield. With his victims scattered and reeling, the Lord of Afflictions descends to wreak havoc. In one hand he carries a festerspike, a long-hafted trident that he stabs viciously at the enemy. With its prongs coated in infectious filth, the slightest cut from one of these weapons is utterly

lethal, instantly becoming thick with oozing pus and squirming maggots. Many of these Lords of Nurgle also carry an incubatch, a rotted corpse that is a hotbed of Nurgle's most virulent diseases.

Contagion spreads outward from those wounded by the Lord of Afflictions with frightening speed. As the Rotbringer lord buzzes skyward once more in search of fresh victims to infect, he leaves in his passing a blossoming epidemic of his god's deadliest plagues, a sight which warms his blackened soul as he soars above the press of combat.

LORDS OF BLIGHTS

A Lord of Blights is a brutish figure who creates and destroys in equal measure. Swollen with muscle, he lumbers into the midst of the foe swinging his bubotic hammer in thunderous arcs. Every impact shatters bone and ruptures organs, leaving his victims lying like bruised and rotten fruit upon the ground. The bludgeoning assault redoubles as the Lord of Blights uses his vermid shield to block incoming blows, before smashing his enemies from their feet with the fly-shaped slab of corroded iron. Yet this brutality has a purpose beyond simple murder.

As he batters his enemies, a Lord of Blights watches for those whose hardy flesh does not rupture beneath his blows, or who withstand his assault for more than a few crushing strikes. Such worthy victims are marked for later and, after the battle, they are gathered up for the sowing to follow.

Using the meat-mulch created by the butchery of battle, and husbanding the plagues that seethe through the remains of the Rotbringers' foes, a Lord of Blights plants corpse orchards. Twisted gallows trees sprout high to blight the land, bearing aloft the bodies of the lord's chosen victims by hempen nooses

set about their necks. Within the head of each cadaver, carefully filled with pus drawn from a Great Unclean One and sealed with a mixture of blood and wax, a batch of virulent disease brews until a new death's head ripens. The readiness of these macabre fruits is shown when the victims' withered bodies drop off to decay at the feet of the gallows trees. At this time, the Lord of Blights harvests his foul crops and distributes them amongst his followers, so that they can be flung at the enemy to detonate in bursts of noxious effluvia. The lord keeps the finest specimens for himself, hanging them from his gallowrack to hurl during battle.

LORDS OF PLAGUES

A Lord of Plagues is a despoiler and a desecrator, who sows rotting filth and sundered corpsemeat across the Mortal Realms by seeking out and hacking down the greatest enemies of his gruesome god. Such champions of Nurgle are typically belligerent and direct, resolutely leading their Cysts to where the fighting is thickest and cleaving apart everything in their path.

These aggressive and unsubtle champions of Nurgle are sometimes known as Festering Headsmen, or the Executioners of Nurgle. Their weapons and bodies alike seethe with disease, which they spread with every blow they strike. A Lord of Plagues even does his god's work through suffering injury, for those enemies who successfully pierce the bloated flesh of such a grotesque champion are rewarded with splattering jets of foulness. Any caught in the spray are infected with everything from Scabrous Squirm to Nurgle's Rot, turning their short-lived victory into a long and agonising defeat.

Meanwhile, the Lord of Plagues hacks and hews at his foes with grim intensity. Some chant as they go about their duties, their macabre intonations carrying over the hideous crunch and splatter of shattered bone and sundered flesh. Every rent corpse he leaves in his wake, every spray of fluids and ruptured organ, is another tilled field ripe for colonisation by Nurgle's diseases.

HARBINGERS OF DECAY

When the evil omen known as Nurgle's Moon hangs tri-lobed and lambent in the sky, the oppressed tribes of the Mortal Realms know an offering must be made to the Plague God. A babe aged seven months and seven days must be taken from its mother and given into the arms of old Grandfather Nurgle. The child is taken to the tribe's shrine and abandoned there. In the morning it is gone, the only clues to its vanishing a trail of sulphurous hoof prints leading away into the wilds.

Some say that it is the Harbingers of Decay that come for the offerings, others that the abandoned infants are destined to become Harbingers themselves, thus inheriting such power that they go beyond the reach of death for evermore. Whatever the truth, these sinister figures are regarded with superstitious fear by even the staunchest Rotbringers, who know them as the Empty Ones, or the Stolen. Slumped beings whose features are hidden in the deep shadows of their cowls, Harbingers ride rotted nags whose hides teem with parasites. Fat flies swarm about them, crawling in and out of their robes, and where their steeds' hooves tread the soil, maggots and worms spill up from the loam.

Harbingers speak but rarely, and when they do their voices sound like the insectile rustle of chitin. All who worship Nurgle attend such utterances well, for it is said that the Harbingers can read the subtle omens in rot and bloat, corrosion and ruin that make their god's desires known. It is a brave or foolhardy Lord who ignores the counsel of his Harbinger, and tales abound of the grisly fates that such heathens have met. Rotbringers fighting beneath the gaze of such a figure battle all the harder, for they feel the eye of Nurgle resting upon them and dread their god's noisome displeasure. Yet such fear is as nothing to the plague of terror that sweeps the enemy's ranks when they face a Harbinger of Nurgle. Leaping from one brave warrior to the next, the Shudderblight pales the flesh, clouds the mind and causes the victim's emotions to manifest physically and rot them from within. Any who survive this dreadful affliction are left weakened and despairing, easy prey for the deadly swing of the Harbinger's scythe.

SORCERERS OF NURGLE

Sorcerers of Nurgle wield the powers of decay, entropy and putrefaction. With a string of glottal curses they can turn their enemies' blood to brackish filth, belch vast clouds of flies or bless their allies with empowering poxes that bloat their bodies and thicken their hides.

Such unnatural powers carry a heavy cost. Many Sorcerers of Nurgle begin as scholarly wizards, or shamans whose magical abilities are derived from the natural energies of the Mortal Realms. Yet in their quest for ever greater knowledge and power, these gifted individuals stray onto the path of damnation. Some seek the might to protect their tribes from harm, or forbidden texts containing the secrets that they believe must surely be of use in the war against Chaos. Others are simply avaricious or incautious, but whatever the case, their fates are the same. One rot-bound tome thrown open beneath the light of a poisoned moon, one lungful of corrupted spores or proscribed incantation uttered, and their soul becomes forfeit. Nurgle takes his due, claiming his new champion and raining down his fecund blessings upon them until they are utterly transformed.

Of course, many Rotbringer Sorcerers rise up from amongst the ranks of the myriad mortal worshippers of Chaos, willingly pledging themselves to Nurgle in exchange for his unnatural gifts. Either way, these beings are grotesque to look upon, their bodies pustule-ridden and crawling with diseased vermin. Many wear mouldering robes, mildewed cloaks and arcane badges of office, and they carry Rotwood staves and satchels of stained scrolls into battle with which to focus their dark powers.

Though at times an especially powerful Sorcerer will lead a Cyst or Contagium to war, many prefer to act as manipulators and counsellors to a suitably powerful lord. Sorcerers supply such a patron with dark lore and esoteric magics to bolster his armies in battle, all the while advancing their own schemes. Like parasites they suckle power from the lands, transmitting Nurgle's plagues in the process.

GUTROT SPUME

Gutrot Spume is a monstrously deformed Rotbringer whose might is matched only by his boundless confidence. Known by many as the Lord of Tentacles, Spume's rotten body reeks of spoiled fish and brine, while the entire left side of his torso is a waving mass of tentacles set around a fang-filled maw. Spume's opponents must contend not only with his inhuman strength and skill, but also with the fleshy tendrils that assail them to ensnare, crush and throttle.

Spume was once a tribal chieftain on the coast of the Ocean of Blades. When the Age of Chaos began he led a hunting fleet in pursuit of a vast rot kraken, hoping to slay the beast and thus impress the gods. Though the monster mauled his fleet, and its young tore his flesh, Spume stabbed the kraken, and was still fighting even as it dragged him down. At that moment, Nurgle saw Spume's potential and blessed him. The Lord of Tentacles rose from the waters as a monstrous champion of Nurgle, dominating the rot kraken with his will and claiming its body as his new lair. Nurgle raised the ships of Spume's hunting fleet, crewed by those who had followed him and who were now elevated to become Putrid Blightkings for their tenacity. Since that day, Gutrot Spume and his fleet have travelled the Mortal Realms, raiding and spreading corruption at will. Spume's flagship is a rotting hulk of gargantuan size that teeters atop the mountainous kraken, while his fleet sails over land and sea alike upon the slime that it leaves in its wake.

FESTUS THE LEECHLORD

The grotesque plague apothecary known as Festus the Leechlord is an almost mythical figure to the Rotbringers. There are those who say that Festus was once a kind and driven healer who sought to defeat the myriad ills assailing mankind. It would prove his undoing. Affronted by the mortal doctor's presumptuousness, Nurgle tormented him with ever more heinous varieties of incurable disease, until at last Festus was driven to the depths of despair. It was then that Nurgle offered him the knowledge that he sought– all it would cost was his soul. Maddened and desperate, Festus accepted, and was forever damned.

Since the Age of Chaos began, Festus has been sighted across the Mortal Realms. Some believe him to be a daemon, others a Rotbringer of exceptional age and malevolence. His coming heralds outbreaks of the most lethal and bizarre plagues, for Festus comes not to conquer in the conventional sense, but to experiment. Just like Grandfather Nurgle himself, Festus delights in the act of creating virulent life and then unleashing it upon the ungrateful foe, brewing magnificent new sicknesses with the aid of his devoted Nurgling assistants, Mucus and Pukus, and singing operatic duets with his favourite leeches as he works.

PUTRID BLIGHTKINGS

Putrid Blightkings are Nurgle's favoured, exceptional mortals who have chosen his worship and been marked by their deity to bear his feculent gifts. They are powerful warriors indeed, for the might of the Plague God clogs their veins.

No Chaos God boasts hardier mortal servants than Nurgle. The Putrid Blightkings are hulking monstrosities, swollen with pus and unnatural vitality. Their bodies are deformed abominations of open wounds and seeping sores, wriggling parasites and spilling innards, yet they know nothing of pain or fatigue.

So hardy are these chosen warriors that they advance relentlessly through the thickest hail of arrows or the most extreme battlefield conditions. They never falter, no matter the projectiles that pepper their rotting hides or the sorcerous flames that lick about

them. Putrid Blightkings take obscene pleasure in soaking up the worst punishment their enemies can mete out, before booming scornful laughs and wading in to crush their foes.

Nurgle values and rewards all who excel in spreading his gifts across the Mortal Realms. Putrid Blightkings are drawn not only from the ranks of warriors and soldiers, but also scholars, surgeons, apothecaries, poets and countless other walks of life. The Blightkings' disgusting appearance is thus counterpointed by a surreal conviviality. They exchange jests, compose revolting verses in praise of

the Plague God's finest blights, and bait their enemies with vivid descriptions of the symptoms they will soon exhibit. None of this takes away from their prowess in battle. The Blightkings swing huge axes, scythes and hammers, smashing their enemies from their feet with ease. They purposefully spit and squirt their rank secretions across their foes, seeking to infect the enemy as much as to slaughter them. Between the horrendous stench that wafts from their decaying bodies, the dolorous toll of rusted bells and the shocking brutality of their attack, it is no wonder many choose to flee rather than face these warriors in battle.

Some Putrid Blightkings choose to undergo a rite known as the Feast of Maggots. Swearing a sevenfold oath to Nurgle upon a site of particularly repulsive corruption, they allow their Cyst's Sorcerer to drop a ravenous slathermaggot into one of their open wounds. This hungry daemon-larva sets to work, chewing its way through the Blightking's necrotic flesh until its body bursts, only to disgorge two identical simulacra of the original maggot.

If left unchecked, the maggots will consume their host within seven days. To avoid this grim fate, the Blightking must seek out the worshippers of Nurgle's brother gods and infect them with the slathermaggot curse. One offering after another must be riddled with parasites, doomed to be devoured as fuel for the spawning of ever more wriggling grubs. Finally, if the

staggering, half-devoured Rotbringer succeeds in infecting seventy-seven foes with his curse, the insects in his body cease eating and congeal into muscle and fat, bulking him out with new putrid might. At the same moment a terrible droning fills the air, and down from on high thrums a Rot Fly, sent by Nurgle as a reward for the Blightking's devotion.

Mounting his new steed, the warrior becomes a Pusgoyle Blightlord, one of Nurgle's elite mortal airborne cavalry. His relationship with the Rot Fly is symbiotic, for the Blightlord vows to protect the spiteful creature with his life and rarely leaves its saddle. This bond helps to anchor the daemonic beast in reality, allowing it to better hunt down its mortal victims without the risk of being drawn back to the Garden of Nurgle. In exchange, the Rot Fly bears its rider faithfully into battle.

Droning bands of Pusgoyle Blightlords form the vanguard of the Rotbringer Contagiums, swooping in low over the enemy with their scythes swinging. Between the powerful blows of the Blightlords themselves and the lashing limbs and biting maws of their mounts, such a band of aerial cavalry can shatter an enemy battle line in a single charge. Like a wound that admits a lethal infection, they tear open a gap for the rest of the Rotbringers to flow into and destroy the foe from the inside out.

To aid in this line-breaking duty, some Blightlords tether dolorous tocsins to the underside of their steed. These huge wrecking bells smash into enemy regiments, scattering serried ranks and shield walls. Such is the weight of their impact that they can even smash barricades to splinters and overturn lumbering war engines, all the while clanging out an infernal din.

VISIONS OF
DECAY

Rotigus Rainfather raises his gnarlrod high as he leads his fellow daemons of Nurgle to conquer the lands.

A Spoilpox Scrivener spews his spiteful vitriol, trying his best to be heard over the manic jollity of a Sloppity Bilepiper.

Beasts of Nurgle bound gleefully into battle, maws slobbering and tentacles spraying paralytic slime.

Rotigus leads a great horde of Nurgle daemons to drive the Stormcast Rangers from the ruins of ancient Oskyr.

Spoilpox Scrivener

Sloppity Bilepiper

Great Unclean One

Horticulous Slimux on Mulch

Plagueridden

Plaguebearer

Icon Bearer

Beast of Nurgle

Beast of Nurgle

Rotbringers pour from a corrupted Realmgate to spread corruption and death amidst the forests of the sylvaneth.

Pusgoyle Blightlords swoop into battle, their revolting steeds drizzling foul fluids as they drone through the skies.

Putrid Blightkings and Pusgoyle Blightlords advance unstoppably into battle, intoning their grim war chants.

The mortal followers of Nurgle rally around the Glottkin, intent on bringing the Plague God's gifts to the realms.

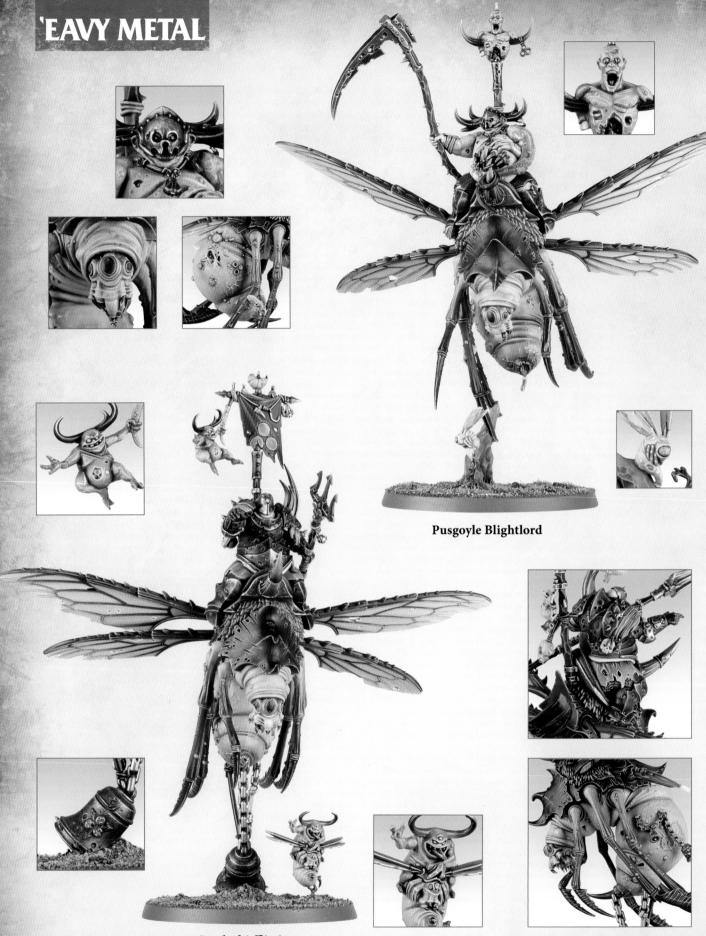

Pusgoyle Blightlord

Lord of Afflictions

Lord of Plagues

Lord of Blights

Gutrot Spume

Putrid Blightking

Putrid Blightking

Putrid Blightking

Putrid Blightking

Putrid Blightking

THE REPUGNANT PARADE

The Repugnant Parade is a Maggotkin army that only recently joined the war for the Mortal Realms. Led by the ever-chortling Great Unclean One Blorx'flogg Bileguts, this foul horde has wasted no time in spreading sickness and despair across the Jade Kingdom of Sede.

Blorx'flogg is a jolly monster, his bloated form quivering with his endless mirth. Every one of his victims' efforts at resistance makes Blorx'flogg laugh out loud, causing tides of giggling Nurglings to shower from the splits in his skin and sheets of rancid bile to spill from his maw and drown his foes. Blorx'flogg's jollity increases yet further at the antics of his Sloppity Bilepiper, Spoughly Spughe, who capers into battle at the head of a daemonic Tallyband. Plaguebearers, Nurgling swarms, Plague Drones and bounding Beasts of Nurgle make up this force, constantly chivvied on by their overseer, the spiteful Spoilpox Scrivener Nux.

Nor do the daemons fight alone. Led by the Lord of Plagues, Sputus Rotspit, the Plague Cyst known as the Gallblades crush their enemies beneath their inexorable advance. They fight hard to prove themselves worthy of Nurgle's gifts, for they are followed into battle by the Harbinger of Decay known as Hope's Shroud. Though this cadaverous figure never speaks, his mere presence is enough to fill his comrades with grim resolve, and their enemies with dread.

1. Great Unclean One
2. Sloppity Bilepiper
3. Spoilpox Scrivener
4. Plaguebearers
5. Plague Drones
6. Nurglings
7. Beasts of Nurgle
8. Lord of Plagues
9. Harbinger of Decay
10. Sorcerer
11. Putrid Blightkings
12. Lord of Afflictions
13. Pusgoyle Blightlords
14. Feculent Gnarlmaw

PAINTING MAGGOTKIN

The hordes of Nurgle offer bountiful opportunities to paint some truly disgusting and characterful models. With a riot of foul and unusual textures, a palette of rot, mould and festering innards, and numerous places to use Citadel Technical paints, painting your Maggotkin is gruesome and fun.

Below you will find a series of easy-to-replicate techniques for painting the foul armour, diseased blades and rancid, blubbery flesh of your Maggotkin. Those with a strong enough stomach will find these tips useful for achieving great results!

ARMOUR

Basecoat with Brass Scorpion, then apply a wash of Reikland Fleshshade. Tidy up the raised areas with more Brass Scorpion, then paint thinned-down Sotek Green into the recesses. Finish with an edge highlight of Stormhost Silver.

Over a Corax White undercoat, apply a layer of Screaming Skull. Shade the recesses with Seraphim Sepia, then highlight the edges with White Scar. For the corrosion, paint thinned-down Rhinox Hide into the pits and recesses.

Start with a basecoat of Castellan Green, then shade the recesses with Reikland Fleshshade. Highlight the edges with lines of Elysian Green, then even thinner lines of Ogryn Camo.

Basecoat with Incubi Darkness, then shade the recesses with Nuln Oil. Apply a two-stage edge highlight, first with Kabalite Green, then with Ogryn Camo. Finish by using Nurgle's Rot to create the effect of slime seeping from the holes.

PLAGUESWORDS

Basecoat Skullcrusher Brass, shade with Agrax Earthshade, edge with Stormhost Silver, then apply dots of Nihilakh Oxide.

Basecoat Abaddon Black, then edge with Sotek Green and Temple Guard Blue. Apply dots of Ulthuan Grey to suggest a shine.

Apply a basecoat of Abaddon Black, then an edge highlight of Ironbreaker. Finish with patches of Nurgle's Rot.

Basecoat Leadbelcher. Shade with Agrax Earthshade then apply Typhus Corrosion and Ryza Rust. Finally, drybrush with Necron Compound.

RUST

Basecoat the metal with Leadbelcher, then follow with an all-over wash of Agrax Earthshade. Apply patches of Ryza Rust, then edge highlight with Stormhost Silver.

GREEN SKIN

First, apply a basecoat of Death Guard Green over a Corax White undercoat.

Next, apply an all-over wash of Athonian Camoshade.

Then, apply a layer of Death Guard Green, leaving the recesses dark.

Lastly, apply an edge highlight of Ogryn Camo to bring out the raised detail.

GREY SKIN

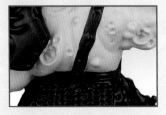  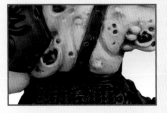 

Apply a basecoat of Celestra Grey over an Abaddon Black undercoat.

Mix Coelia Greenshade and Lahmian Medium and apply as an all-over wash.

Once the shade has completely dried, apply a layer of Celestra Grey.

Use Ulthuan Grey to apply an edge highlight to the raised areas.

DETAILS

Basecoat the exposed innards with Cadian Fleshtone.

Apply a layer of Blood for the Blood God to achieve this revolting effect.

To make your models' buboes look slimy, apply Nurgle's Rot to them.

Use a dot of Ungor Flesh to make the buboes stand out and look ready to pop.

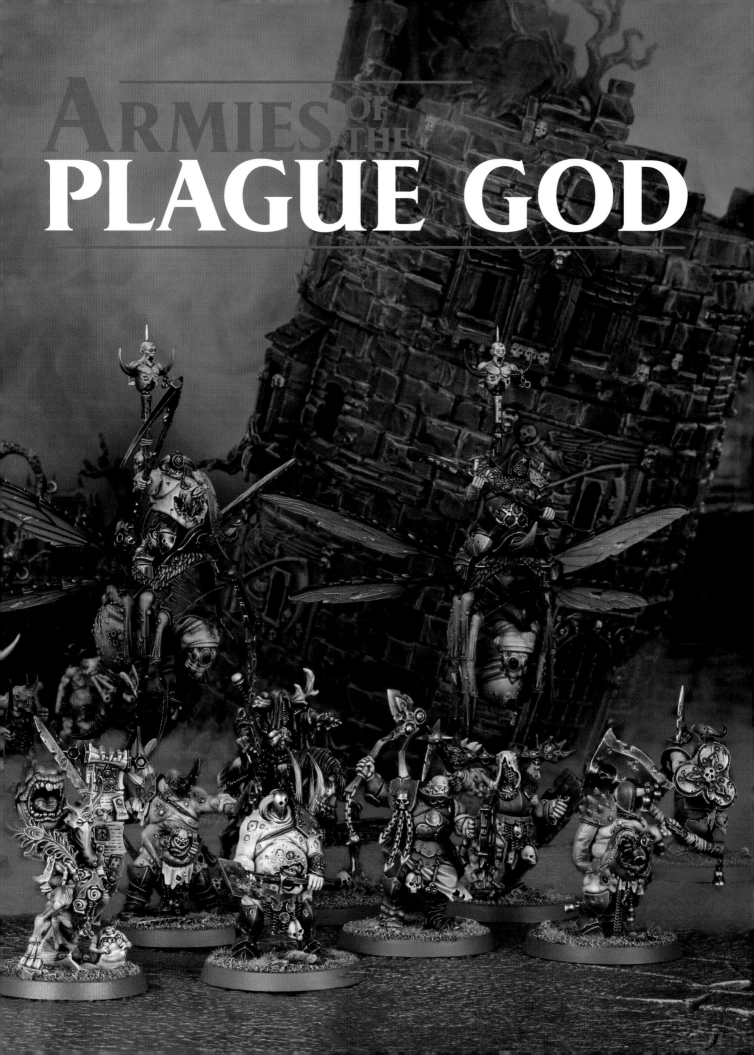

ARMIES OF THE PLAGUE GOD

FORCES OF NURGLE

On the following pages you will find exciting rules for your Nurgle army. These include powerful allegiance abilities and items, a new battleplan and scenery model, and warscrolls and battalions that describe the unwholesome forces of the Plague God in games of *Warhammer Age of Sigmar*.

ALLEGIANCE ABILITIES

From the foul blessings granted by Nurgle to revolting artefacts of incredible virulence, this section provides rules and abilities for the Plague God's armies.

ALLEGIANCE

When you choose your army, you can also choose an allegiance for it. If you do so, you can use the allegiance abilities that correspond to the allegiance you have chosen.

On the following pages you will find a set of allegiance abilities that can be used for an army that has the NURGLE allegiance. In order to have the NURGLE allegiance, all of the units in the army must either have the NURGLE keyword, or be assigned the NURGLE keyword during set-up.

If an army could have more than one allegiance, you must pick one to apply to it during the game. The allegiance you choose will apply for the duration of the battle, even if you add new units to the army during the battle that have a different allegiance.

Battle Traits: An allied army fights with unity and cohesion, granting it additional boons. See pages 59-61 for the battle traits available to a NURGLE army.

Command Traits: Each leader has their own style of command. See page 62 for the command traits available to NURGLE generals.

Artefacts of Power: These profane treasures and blessings are borne by Nurgle's mightiest champions. See pages 63-65 for the artefacts your army can be gifted.

The Lores of Nurgle: Nurgle's minions can unleash powerful magic to overwhelm, corrupt and destroy their victims. See pages 66-67 for the spells available to WIZARDS from a NURGLE army.

NAMED CHARACTERS

Rotigus, Epidemius, Horticulous Slimux, the Glottkin, Orghotts Daemonspew, Bloab Rotspawned, Morbidex Twiceborn, Festus the Leechlord and Gutrot Spume are singular and powerful champions of Nurgle with their own unique personalities and bespoke items of terrible potency. As such, these models cannot have a command trait or artefact of power.

BATTLEPLAN

The battleplan on page 74 allows you to fight a battle based on the tactics that Nurgle's followers use in war.

PATH TO GLORY

On pages 68-73 you will find rules for playing a Path to Glory campaign. Included are warband tables to help you collect your army and a warband roster you can use in your games.

WARSCROLL BATTALIONS

Pages 78-85 describe formations made up of several units that combine their strengths to gain powerful new abilities. There are rules for fielding some of the most renowned warbands and daemonic hosts, each possessing its own strengths and distinct character.

WARSCROLLS

Pages 86-103 describe the characteristics and abilities of the individual units that form a NURGLE army.

MOUNTS

Some heroes have a mount that they can ride. In such cases, any command traits or magical artefacts can only be used to affect attacks made by the hero, and have no effect on attacks made by their mount unless specifically stated otherwise.

ALLEGIANCE ABILITIES

A Nurgle army is a revolting sight, a relentless horde of diseased warriors that pervert the natural order by spreading corruption and decay. This section describes the battle traits that a Nurgle army possesses, and the command traits that its general can have.

BATTLE TRAITS

A Nurgle army has the following battle traits:

Cycle of Corruption: Nurgle's power and blessings follow a never-ending cycle of fecundity and decay.

Roll a dice at the start of the first battle round of any battle that includes any Nurgle armies, before rolling to see who has the first turn. Refer to the table opposite to see which stage of the Cycle of Corruption is currently taking place – this applies to all Nurgle armies. The Cycle of Corruption moves clockwise one step at the start of each new battle round. For example, if the roll on the Cycle of Corruption table was a 5, then Nauseous Revulsion would apply in the first battle round, Rampant Disease in the second, Corrupted Regrowth in the third, and so on. The rule for the current stage applies for the duration of the battle round.

D6	Stage of Corruption
1	Unnatural Vitality
2	Fecund Vigour
3	The Burgeoning
4	Plague of Misery
5	Nauseous Revulsion
6	Rampant Disease

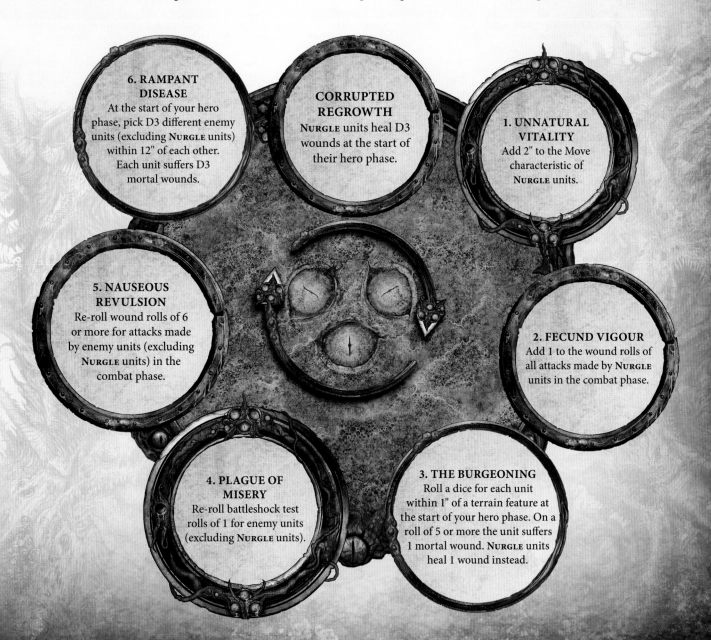

6. RAMPANT DISEASE
At the start of your hero phase, pick D3 different enemy units (excluding Nurgle units) within 12" of each other. Each unit suffers D3 mortal wounds.

CORRUPTED REGROWTH
Nurgle units heal D3 wounds at the start of their hero phase.

1. UNNATURAL VITALITY
Add 2" to the Move characteristic of Nurgle units.

5. NAUSEOUS REVULSION
Re-roll wound rolls of 6 or more for attacks made by enemy units (excluding Nurgle units) in the combat phase.

2. FECUND VIGOUR
Add 1 to the wound rolls of all attacks made by Nurgle units in the combat phase.

4. PLAGUE OF MISERY
Re-roll battleshock test rolls of 1 for enemy units (excluding Nurgle units).

3. THE BURGEONING
Roll a dice for each unit within 1" of a terrain feature at the start of your hero phase. On a roll of 5 or more the unit suffers 1 mortal wound. Nurgle units heal 1 wound instead.

The Garden of Nurgle: When the armies of Nurgle march to war, their filth and corruption causes Feculent Gnarlmaws to burst from the soil, revolting trees from the Realm of Chaos which attract the Plague God's daemons.

After all other terrain features are set up, but before you choose a territory or set up your army, you can set up one Feculent Gnarlmaw (pg 103) anywhere on the battlefield that is more than 1" from any other terrain feature. If both players can set up a Feculent Gnarlmaw, each player rolls a dice, rolling again in the case of a tie, and whoever rolls higher can choose the order in which the Feculent Gnarlmaws are set up.

Summon Daemons of Nurgle: Areas of the Mortal Realms that are overrun by Nurgle's minions become weak points in reality through which his daemons can be drawn from the Realm of Chaos.

You can summon units of **Nurgle Daemons** to the battlefield if you collect enough contagion points. At the start of each of your hero phases, you receive 3 contagion points if there are any friendly **Nurgle** models in your own territory, and 3 additional contagion points if there are any friendly **Nurgle** models in your opponent's territory. If there are no enemy models in the same territory as friendly **Nurgle** models, you receive 1 extra contagion point for that territory. In addition, you receive D3 contagion points for each Feculent Gnarlmaw that has no enemy models within 3" of it.

If you have 7 or more contagion points at the end of your movement phase, you can summon one or more units from the following list to the battlefield, and add them to your army. Each unit you summon costs a number of contagion points, as shown on the list, and you can only summon a unit if you have enough contagion points remaining to pay its cost.

Summoned units must be set up wholly within 12" of a Feculent Gnarlmaw or a friendly **Nurgle Hero**, and more than 9" from any enemy models. If the summoned unit is a Feculent Gnarlmaw, it must also be set up more than 1" from any terrain features. Subtract the cost of the summoned unit from the number of contagion points you have available immediately after it has been set up.

Unit	Cost
1 Great Unclean One	28
1 Horticulous Slimux	21
3 Plague Drones	21
20 Plaguebearers	21
1 Poxbringer, Herald of Nurgle	14
1 Sloppity Bilepiper, Herald of Nurgle	14
1 Spoilpox Scrivener, Herald of Nurgle	14
10 Plaguebearers	14
1 Beast of Nurgle	14
3 Nurgling bases	14
5 Plaguebearers	7
1 Nurgling base	7
1 Feculent Gnarlmaw	7

'When the plague moon bloats up fat like Nurgle's jaundiced eye, when the Maggotkin go a-marching, and the mists churn foetid moist, then can the daemons of the Plague God be beckoned hence to walk the realms.

Firstly should ye dig the Filth Pits, the tri-lobe deeps all wriggling a-rotten, and slickenslop their walls. Take the unfaithful, the fools that live and them that do not, and cast them hence unto the tripletmaw, to wallow there 'midst the blessed sludge.

Speak ye then the seven incantations of plentiful rot. Intone the dirge of the bubotic blessing, and vomit the urging prayer. Let the words of Nurgle drip like pus from thy rotted gums, 'til they gather miasmal all about.

Dance then, though your bones might creak and your plumpened blisters burst, for Nurgle delights in a revel. Toll the bells of welcome 'round the Gnarlmaw trees, and cry out praise 'midst the shrilling of the maggots and the droning of the flies. Then does the mouldering curtain part, and rustengate creak open to the Garden Glorisome. Then shall the Tallybands trudge out, to bear Grandfather's givings hence. Then shall the blessings of Nurgle be upon thee, and his fulsome gratitude be thine.

Give praise! Give praise! Give praise! The daemons of Nurgle are come!'

- Gulthrox the Festerling, On Summoning Ye the Daemons of the Grandfather

COMMAND TRAITS

If the general of a NURGLE army is a HERO, they can have one of the following command traits. Depending on whether your general is a ROTBRINGER, DAEMON or MORTAL, you must select the trait from the Rotbringer, Nurgle Daemon or Nurgle Mortal table respectively (if they qualify for more than one table, pick which one to use). You can either pick the trait or roll a dice to randomly determine it. If, for any reason, you must select a new general during a battle, immediately generate a trait for them.

ROTBRINGER

D6	Command Trait
1	**Grandfather's Blessing:** Once per battle, at the start of your hero phase, you can move the Cycle of Corruption one stage forward or backward if your general has not been slain.
2	**Living Plague:** At the start of your hero phase, roll a dice for each enemy unit within 1" of your general. On a 4+ the unit being rolled for suffers 1 mortal wound and you receive 1 contagion point.
3	**Hulking Physique:** Add 1 to wound rolls for your general in the combat phase.
4	**Bloated with Corruption:** Roll a dice each time you allocate a wound to your general in the combat phase (and it is not negated). On a 4+ the attacking unit suffers 1 mortal wound after all of its attacks have been made.
5	**Avalanche of Rotten Flesh:** Add 2 to run and charge rolls for your general.
6	**Resilient:** Roll a dice each time you allocate a wound or mortal wound to your general. On a 6+ the wound is negated.

NURGLE DAEMON

D6	Command Trait
1	**Grandfather's Blessing:** Once per battle, at the start of your hero phase, you can move the Cycle of Corruption one stage forward or backward if your general has not been slain.
2	**Living Plague:** At the start of your hero phase, roll a dice for each enemy unit within 1" of your general. On a 4+ the unit being rolled for suffers 1 mortal wound and you receive 1 contagion point.
3	**Hulking Physique:** Add 1 to wound rolls for your general in the combat phase.
4	**Tainted Corruptor:** At the start of each of your hero phases, you can pick one terrain feature that is within 3" of your general. For the rest of the battle, that terrain feature has the Sickness Blossoms scenery rule from the Feculent Gnarlmaw warscroll (pg 103), in addition to any other rules it already had.
5	**Nurgling Infestation:** Once per battle, at the start of a combat phase, you can inflict D3 mortal wounds on an enemy unit that is within 3" of your general.
6	**Pestilent Breath:** At the start of your shooting phase, pick one enemy unit within 6" of your general. Roll a dice for each model in that unit that is within 6" of your general. The unit suffers 1 mortal wound for each roll of 5+.

NURGLE MORTAL

D6	Command Trait
1	**Grandfather's Blessing:** Once per battle, at the start of your hero phase, you can move the Cycle of Corruption one stage forward or backward if your general has not been slain.
2	**Living Plague:** At the start of your hero phase, roll a dice for each enemy unit within 1" of your general. On a 4+ the unit being rolled for suffers 1 mortal wound and you receive 1 contagion point.
3	**Hulking Physique:** Add 1 to wound rolls for your general in the combat phase.
4	**Hideous Visage:** Subtract 2 from the Bravery characteristic of enemy units while they are within 3" of your general.
5	**Overpowering Stench:** Re-roll hit rolls of 6+ for attacks that target your general in the combat phase.
6	**Virulent Contagion:** Improve the Rend characteristic by 1 for attacks made by your general in the combat phase.

ARTEFACTS OF POWER

If a **Nurgle** army includes any **Heroes**, one may bear one of the following artefacts of power. Depending on whether the **Hero** is a **Rotbringer**, **Daemon** or **Mortal**, you must select the artefact from the Artefacts of Contagion, Daemonic Boons or Plagueridden Gifts table respectively (if they qualify for more than one table, pick which one to use). You can either pick the artefact, or roll a dice to randomly determine it. You may choose one additional **Hero** to have an artefact for each warscroll battalion you include in your army. A **Hero** cannot have more than one artefact of power, and an army may not include duplicates of the same artefact of power.

ARTEFACTS OF CONTAGION

Any **Rotbringer Hero** can be given one of the following artefacts of contagion.

D6 Artefact

1 **The Splithorn Helm:** This rusted helm was scrimshawed from a shed chunk of a Great Unclean One's antler. Daemonic energies still linger around it, blessing its wearer with supernatural resilience.

Roll a dice each time you allocate a wound or mortal wound to the bearer. On a 6+ the wound is negated.

2 **Muttergrub:** A daemonic familiar prised from the Rotwood joists of Nurgle's Manse, this bloated maggot curls itself within its master's ear and mumbles the secrets of Nurgle's magic to them.

If the bearer is a **Wizard**, they can attempt to cast one additional spell in each of their hero phases. If the bearer is not a **Wizard**, they can attempt to cast Foul Regenesis (pg 66) in each of their hero phases (this does not give them the ability to unbind spells).

3 **Rustfang:** Rustfang is a cursed battle-axe whose blade crawls with a thick layer of sentient corrosion. The slightest touch of this blade spreads its ferric blight, chewing away the foe's armour in moments.

At the start of the combat phase, pick one enemy unit within 3" of the bearer. Subtract 1 from its save rolls for the rest of the battle. You cannot use this ability more than once on the same enemy unit.

4 **Flesh Pealer:** This cursed bell was dredged up from the depths of the Festerswamp. When tolled, the bell emits waves of sorcerous energy that slough flesh from bone and rot living victims into heaps of slime.

In your hero phase, roll a dice for each enemy unit that is within 6" of the bearer. On a 5+ the unit being rolled for suffers D3 mortal wounds.

5 **The Bileheart:** Originally a sylvaneth soulpod, this foul artefact was cursed by Golgous the Bitter. It is forcibly thrust into the bearer's chest, where it takes root and pumps ichor through their veins that spurts out in infectious gouts should they be wounded.

Roll a dice each time you allocate a wound or mortal wound to the bearer in the combat phase (and it is not negated). On a 4+ the attacking unit suffers 1 mortal wound after all of its attacks have been made.

6 **The Fecund Flask:** It is said that an entire ocean of infectious waters was trammelled within this grimy glass bottle. Its bearer can drink deep of its endless flow, allowing the poisonous blessings of Nurgle to restore their vitality – though not always in the way the drinker may have hoped.

You can use the fecund flask once per battle, at the start of your hero phase. If you do so, roll a dice. On a 2+ any wounds the bearer has suffered are healed. On a 1, the bearer is slain. If the bearer is slain by the fecund flask, before you remove the bearer's model, you can add a Beast of Nurgle to your army and set it up within 1" of the bearer.

DAEMONIC BOONS

Any **NURGLE DAEMON HERO** can be given one of the following Daemonic Boons.

D6 Artefact

1 Noxious Nexus: This daemon is a festering carrier for literally thousands of Nurgle's most virulent plagues. Simply to stand near them risks a myriad of horrible fates, each more revolting and agonising than the last.

At the start of your hero phase, roll a dice for each enemy unit within 7" of the bearer. If the roll is equal to or less than the number of the current battle round, the unit being rolled for suffers 1 mortal wound. For example, in the second battle round, enemy units would suffer a mortal wound on a 1 or 2.

2 Nurgle's Nail: Rumour has it that this plaguesword was fashioned from a splinter of one of Nurgle's own toenails. The foulness that drizzles from its blade is so infectious that it rots reality itself, and can reduce its victims to blackened sludge in seconds.

Pick one of the bearer's melee weapons to be Nurgle's Nail. At the end of each combat phase, roll 2D6 for each enemy model that was allocated any wounds caused by Nurgle's Nail in that phase and was not slain. If the result is exactly 7, the model being rolled for is slain. Any other result has no effect.

3 The Bountiful Swarm: A cloud of cheerfully buzzing flies surrounds this daemon at all times, their bodies the lurid green of infected pus. Those they sting find Nurgle's gifts flowing into them in an uncontrolled flood, causing their bodies to swell with mutation and disease until they devolve into spawn, or simply burst like overripe fruit.

At the start of your hero phase, pick an enemy model within 3" of the bearer and then roll a dice. If the roll is greater than that model's Wounds characteristic, then it is slain. If a model with a Wounds characteristic of 4+ is slain by the Bountiful Swarm, before you remove the model, you can add a Beast of Nurgle to your army and set it up within 1" of the enemy model.

4 The Witherstave: Carved from the heartwood of a tormented Treelord, the Witherstave thrums with a soured mockery of the sylvaneth spirit song. Those struck with it feel a terrible weakness shiver their limbs as a jarring dirge of despair clouds their minds.

Re-roll hit rolls of 6 for enemy units while they are within 12" of the bearer.

5 Tome of a Thousand Poxes: This rotting book is so bloated that it requires a trio of chattering Nurglings to carry it into battle. Its groaning pages are thick with foul secrets of sorcerous plague lore that can reduce Dreadforts to tumbled ruin and enemy armies to heaps of flyblown corpses.

If the bearer is a **WIZARD**, add 1 to the casting rolls for any spells from the Lore of Nurgle that they attempt to cast. If the bearer is not a **WIZARD**, they can attempt to cast the Sumptuous Pestilence spell (pg 67) in each of your hero phases (they cannot unbind spells).

6 The Endless Gift: Whenever this daemon is injured by its foes, bilious flab and scuttling parasites spill from the wounds. These heap into layers of new growth before crusting over and solidifying into unnatural flesh, leaving the daemon healed as though it had never been harmed at all.

At the start of the battleshock phase, roll a dice for each wound that was allocated to this model during the same turn. On a 4+ the wound is healed.

PLAGUERIDDEN GIFTS

Any **Nurgle Mortal Hero** can be given one of the following Plagueridden Gifts.

D6 Artefact

1 The Virulent Blade: This blotched and rusting sword seethes with magical contagions that it spreads through the enemy ranks with every blow. As its wielder hacks his way across the battlefield, he leaves outbreaks of disease spreading in his wake.

Pick one of the bearer's melee weapons to be the Virulent Blade. Add 1 to the Damage characteristic for attacks made with the Virulent Blade if the wound roll for the attack is 5+.

2 The Foetid Shroud: This mildewed cloak clings to its wearer's body as though drenched in fever-sweat. Enemies find themselves entangled in its clammy folds, their blows reduced to a fumbling struggle to escape the shroud's sopping grasp.

Re-roll hit rolls of 6+ or more for attacks that target the bearer in the combat phase.

3 Sublucus' Stenchplate: This verdigrised suit of Chaos armour is infused with a stench so wretched that even Nurgle's daemons cannot adequately describe it. Enemies recoil, choking on their own vomit, at its slightest whiff, or simply pass out altogether as their senses are overwhelmed.

Enemy units that are within 3" of the bearer at the end of their movement phase suffer D3 mortal wounds.

4 The Eye of Nurgle: This ancient bronze amulet is inscribed with a tri-lobed keyhole, through which Nurgle himself occasionally peeks with one vast, rheumy eye. Should an enemy be unlucky enough to stand before the bearer at such a time, they are damned in an instant, overwhelmed by the Plague God's noxious gifts.

Once per battle, at the start of your hero phase, you can roll 2D6 if there are any enemy models within 12" of the bearer. If the result is exactly 7, then the closest enemy model to the bearer is slain.

5 The Carrion Dirge: A spiralling horn torn from the skull of a Pestigor chieftain, when winded this awful object emits the cawing shrieks of a thousand starving carrion birds. So dreadful is this sound that it can break the spirit of the enemy, and leave them cowering on their knees.

Subtract 2 from the Bravery characteristic of enemy units while they are within 12" of the bearer.

6 The Shield of Growths: This revolting shield is fashioned from diseased troggoth flesh grown around a frame of rusted iron. The more damage it takes, the more it regrows, bulging outward into a ponderous bulwark of rotting blubber and skin.

You can re-roll failed save rolls for the bearer if the roll is equal to or less than the number of wounds currently allocated to the bearer.

THE LORES OF NURGLE

The magic used by the followers of Nurgle centres around corruption, disease, decay and regrowth – those proficient in its use can cause terrible harm to those who stand against them in battle.

All **Wizards** in a **Nurgle** army know the Foul Regenesis spell to the right, in addition to any other spells that they know.

Each **Wizard** in a **Nurgle** army also knows one spell from one of the Lores of Nurgle. Depending on whether the Wizard is a **Rotbringer**, **Daemon** or **Mortal**, you must select the spell from the Lore of Malignance, Lore of Virulence or Lore of Foulness table

respectively (if they qualify for more than one table, pick which one to use). You can either pick the spell, or roll a D3 to randomly determine it.

FOUL REGENESIS

The wizard beseeches the Plague God to begin the Cycle of Corruption anew.

Foul Regenesis has a casting value of 7. If successfully cast, pick a result from the Stage of Corruption table (pg 59) – the Cycle of Corruption is immediately reset to the stage you picked.

LORE OF MALIGNANCE
Any **Rotbringer Wizard** can know one of the following spells.

1. BLADES OF PUTREFACTION
The wizard blesses weapons so that they ooze with the choicest of Nurgle's foul contagions.

Blades of Putrefaction has a casting value of 7. If successfully cast, pick a friendly unit within 14" of the caster that is visible to them. Until your next hero phase, hit rolls of 6+ for that unit inflict 1 mortal wound in addition to any other damage.

2. RANCID VISITATIONS
As the wizard reaches out, their enemies are seized by a terrible affliction that blackens their flesh and rots their organs to mulch.

Rancid Visitations has a casting value of 6. If successfully cast, pick an enemy unit within 3" of the caster. That unit suffers 1 mortal wound for each model from the unit that is within 3" of the caster.

3. GIFT OF CONTAGION
With a gesture the wizard smothers his enemies in a foul fog buzzing with daemon-flies and suffused with enfeebling airborne diseases.

Gift of Contagion has a casting value of 6. If successfully cast, select an enemy unit within 18" of the caster that is visible to them. Then roll a dice and look up the result on the table below. Apply the penalty to all models in the unit until the start of your next hero phase.

D6	Result
1-2	**Flyblown Palsy:** Subtract 1 from the unit's hit rolls in the combat phase.
3-4	**Muscular Atrophy:** Subtract 1 from the unit's wound rolls in the combat phase.
5-6	**Liquefying Ague:** Subtract 1 from the unit's save rolls.

LORE OF VIRULENCE

Any **Nurgle Daemon Wizard** can know one of the following spells.

1. FAVOURED POXES

Calling upon Nurgle to bless his enemies, the daemon concentrates his attentions on an enemy, inflicting wave after wave of debilitating sickness upon them.

Favoured Poxes has a casting value of 7. If successfully cast, pick an enemy unit within 14" of the caster that is visible to them. Subtract 1 from hit, wound and save rolls for that unit until the caster moves, attempts to cast a spell or is slain.

2. GLORIOUS AFFLICTIONS

Hawking a wad of cloudy phlegm, the daemon picks a foe to be infected with an atrophying canker that twists limbs and withers their muscles, making any movement horribly painful.

Glorious Afflictions has a casting value of 5. If successfully cast, pick an enemy unit within 21" of the caster that is visible to them. The unit's Move characteristic and any run or charge rolls made for them are halved (rounding up) until your next hero phase. In addition, units that can normally fly cannot do so until your next hero phase.

3. SUMPTUOUS PESTILENCE

Virulent plagues erupt across the entire battlefield as the daemon recites all of the diseases it has been blessed with during its millennia of service to Nurgle.

Sumptuous Pestilence has a casting value of 6. If successfully cast, each enemy unit within 7" of the caster suffers 1 mortal wound. Units with more than 5 models suffer D3 mortal wounds instead.

LORE OF FOULNESS

Any **Nurgle Mortal Wizard** can know one of the following spells.

1. MAGNIFICENT BUBOES

With a gracious sweep of his hand, the Sorcerer bestows upon his victim one of Nurgle's prettiest afflictions – a clutch of debilitating pustules and boils.

Magnificent Buboes has a casting value of 7. If successfully cast, pick an enemy **Hero** within 21" of the caster that is visible to them. The hero suffers D3 mortal wounds. In addition, subtract 1 from their hit rolls, casting rolls and unbinding rolls until your next hero phase.

2. PLAGUE SQUALL

Singing an extravagant prayer to Grandfather Nurgle, the Sorcerer causes the skies to split open like the swollen belly of a corpse, raining a glorious shower of boiling filth upon his foes.

Plague Squall has a casting value of 6. If successfully cast, roll 7 dice. For each roll of 6, you can pick an enemy unit that is visible to the caster. That unit suffers D3 mortal wounds. If you roll more than one 6, you must pick a different enemy unit to suffer each set of mortal wounds.

3. CLOYING QUAGMIRE

The Sorcerer thrusts his hands into the soil, causing the ground to putrefy into a sucking, grasping quagmire.

Cloying Quagmire has a casting value of 5. If successfully cast, select an enemy unit within 14" of the caster that is visible to them. Then roll a dice, and compare it to the enemy unit's Save characteristic. If the roll is equal to or higher than the Save characteristic, the unit suffers D6 mortal wounds.

PATH TO GLORY CAMPAIGNS

Path to Glory campaigns centre around collecting and fighting battles with a warband in the Age of Sigmar. Champions fight each other and gather followers to join them in their quest for glory, taking advantage of this age of unending battle to win great renown.

In order to take part in a Path to Glory campaign, you will need two or more players. All players will need to have at least one **Hero**, who is their champion, and must then create a warband to follow and fight beside their champion during the campaign.

The players fight battles against each other using the warbands they have created. The results of these battles will gain their warband favour. The warband will swell in numbers as more warriors flock to their banner, while existing troops become more powerful.

After gaining enough favour or growing your warband enough to dominate all others through sheer weight of numbers, you will be granted a final test. Succeed, and your glory will be affirmed for all time, and you will be crowned as the victor of the campaign.

CREATING A WARBAND

When creating a Path to Glory warband, do not select your army in the normal manner. Instead, your army consists of a mighty champion battling to earn the favour of the gods, and their entire band of loyal followers. As you wage war against other warbands, your own warband will grow, and existing units will become grizzled veterans.

WARBAND ROSTER

The details and progress of each warband need to be recorded on a warband roster, which you can download for free from games-workshop.com.

To create a warband, simply follow these steps and record the results on your warband roster:

1. First, pick an allegiance for your warband. Each allegiance has its own set of warband tables that are used to generate the units in the warband and the rewards they can receive for fighting battles. The warband tables included in this battletome let you collect a warband with the **Rotbringer** or **Nurgle Daemon** allegiance, but other *Warhammer Age of Sigmar* publications include warband tables to let you collect other warbands from the Grand Alliances of **Order**, **Chaos**, **Death** and **Destruction**.

2. Next, choose your warband's champion by selecting one of the options from your allegiance's champion table. The champion you choose will determine the number of followers in your warband. Give your champion a suitably grand name, and write this down on your warband roster.

3. Having picked your champion, the next step is to generate your starting followers. These can be chosen from the followers tables for your allegiance. If your allegiance has more than one followers table you can freely choose which ones you use, selecting all of your followers from a single table or from several. Instead of choosing, you can place your destiny in the hands of fate and roll on the followers tables instead. To make a followers roll, pick a column from one of the followers tables and then roll a dice.

4. Your followers need to be organised into units. The follower table tells you how many models the unit has. Follower units cannot include additional models, but they can otherwise take any options listed on their warscroll. Chaos warband followers can only be given the mark of their champion's patron. Record all of the information about your followers on your warband roster.

5. Instead of generating a unit of followers, your champion can start the campaign with a Champion's Reward, or one of your units can start with a Follower's Reward. No champion or unit can start the Path to Glory campaign with more than one reward each.

6. Finally, give your warband a name, one that will inspire respect and dread in your rivals. Your warband is now complete, and you can fight your first battle. Good luck!

TO WAR!

Having created a warband, you can now fight battles with it against other warbands taking part in the campaign. You can fight battles as and when you wish, and can use any of the battleplans available for *Warhammer Age of Sigmar*. There are some battleplans, for example in the *General's Handbook*, that have been designed specifically for use in Path to Glory campaigns.

The units you use for a game must be those on your roster. Units can either be fielded at their full roster strength, or broken down into smaller units, as long as no unit is smaller than the minimum size shown on its warscroll.

Any casualties suffered by a warband are assumed to have been replaced in time for its next battle. If your champion is slain in a battle, it is assumed that they were merely injured, and they are back to full strength for your next game, thirsty for vengeance!

GAINING GLORY

All of the players in the campaign are vying for glory. The amount of glory they have received is represented by the Glory Points that the warband has accumulated. Glory can be increased by fighting and winning battles, as described next. As a warband's glory increases, it will also attract additional followers, and a warband's champion may be granted rewards.

Warbands receive Glory Points after a battle is complete. If the warband drew or lost the battle, it receives 1 Glory Point. If it won the battle, it receives D3 Glory Points (re-roll a result of 1 on the D3 if you won a **major victory**).

Add the Glory Points you scored to the total recorded on your roster. Once you have won 10 Glory Points, you will have a chance to win the campaign, as described below.

REWARDS OF BATTLE

Each allegiance has its own set of rewards tables. After each battle you can take one of the three following options. Alternatively, roll a dice to determine which option to take (1-2 = Additional Followers, 3-4 = Champion's Reward, 5-6 = Follower's Reward).

1 **Additional Followers:** More followers flock to your banner. Either select a new unit or roll for a random one from a follower table, then add it to your warband roster. You can choose from any of your own follower tables, or from any of the follower tables from an allied warband table i.e. a warband table whose allegiance is from the same Grand Alliance as your own. In either case, if you wish to add a unit from a follower table that requires more than '1 roll', you must also reduce your Glory Points total by 1 (if you do not have enough Glory Points, you cannot choose a unit from such a table). Once 5 new units have joined your warband, you will have a chance to win the campaign, as described below.

2 **Champion's Reward:** Your champion's prowess grows. Roll on your allegiance's champion rewards table. Note the result on your warband roster. If you roll a result the champion has already received, roll again until you get a different result.

3 **Follower's Reward:** Your warriors become renowned for mighty deeds. Pick a unit of followers (not one from an allied warband table), then roll on your allegiance's followers rewards table. Note the result on your warband roster. If you roll a result the unit has already received, roll again until you get a different result.

ETERNAL GLORY

There are two ways to win a Path to Glory campaign; either by Blood or by Might. To win by Blood your warband must first have 10 Glory Points. To win by Might your warband must have at least 5 additional units of followers. In either case, you must then fight and win one more battle to win the campaign. If the next battle you fight is tied or lost, you do not receive any Glory Points – just keep on fighting battles until you either win the campaign… or another player wins first!

You can shorten or lengthen a campaign by lowering or raising the number of Glory Points needed to win by Blood, or the numbers of extra units that must join it to win by Might. For example, for a shorter campaign, you could say that a warband only needs 5 Glory Points before the final fight, or for a longer one, say that 15 are needed.

NURGLE WARBAND TABLES

Use the following tables to determine the champion that leads your warband, the followers that make up the units which fight at their side, and the rewards they can receive after battle.

CHAMPION TABLE

Champion	Followers
Great Unclean One	2 units
Harbinger of Decay	4 units
Lord of Afflictions	3 units
Lord of Blights/Lord of Plagues	4 units
Sorcerer	4 units
Herald of Nurgle (any type)	4 units

RETINUE FOLLOWERS TABLE

D6	Followers
1	3 Nurgling bases
2	10 Plaguebearers
3	10 Plaguebearers
4	10 Plaguebearers
5	10 Plaguebearers
6	1 Beast of Nurgle

HERO FOLLOWERS TABLE

D6	Rotbringers	Daemons
1-2	1 Sorcerer	1 Poxbringer, Herald of Nurgle
3	1 Harbinger of Decay	1 Spoilpox Scrivener, Herald of Nurgle
4	1 Lord of Blights	1 Spoilpox Scrivener, Herald of Nurgle
5	1 Lord of Plagues	1 Sloppity Bilepiper, Herald of Nurgle
6	1 Lord of Afflictions	1 Sloppity Bilepiper, Herald of Nurgle

ELITE RETINUE FOLLOWERS TABLE

(uses 2 rolls, or 1 roll and 1 Glory Point)

D6	Rotbringers	Daemons
1-2	5 Putrid Blightkings	3 Plague Drones
3-4	5 Putrid Blightkings	3 Plague Drones
5-6	2 Pusgoyle Blightlords	3 Plague Drones

FOLLOWERS REWARDS TABLE

As your warband progresses along the Path to Glory, it will attract more followers, and especially favoured units will become renowned across the Mortal Realms.

D6 Reward

1 **Driven by Devotion:** Once per battle, in your hero phase, you can declare that this unit will prove their devotion to your champion. You can re-roll failed hit rolls for the unit for the rest of the turn.

2 **Unnatural Regeneration:** In each of your hero phases, you can heal one wound that has been allocated to a model in this unit.

3 **Boon of Virulence:** Once per battle, in your hero phase, you can bestow Nurgle's foetid blessings upon this unit's weapons. You can re-roll any failed wound rolls for the unit in the combat phase of that turn.

4 **Revolting Resilience:** Once per battle, in your hero phase, you can choose for this unit to ignore all but the most grievous of injuries. Improve this unit's Save characteristic by 1 until the start of your next turn.

5 **Gift of Life:** Once per battle, in your hero phase, you can roll a dice for each model in this unit that has been slain. On a result of 5 or 6, return the model to the unit.

6 **Twice-blessed Followers:** Roll twice on this table and apply both results. Re-roll duplicates and further rolls of 6.

DESIGNER'S NOTE

The Path to Glory rules presented in this book allow you to play an exciting campaign with your friends. You can use the rules exactly as they are laid out here, and fight your way along your path to glory! However, you can instead look at these rules as a framework that you can tinker with however you like, to play the campaign that works best for you and your gaming group.

For example, if you're starting new armies, you might start the campaign with fewer followers – perhaps your general and just two or three other units – that will allow everyone to start playing battles a bit sooner. If, on the other hand, your gaming group is looking for a new challenge, you could decide to generate all followers randomly, taking away the option to choose each unit.

You can take things further – there's nothing to stop you writing your own battleplans to use in your Path to Glory campaigns, or adapting the rules from the *General's Handbook* to play battles with three or more players in your campaign. Equally, while we've said that you can adjust the number of Glory Points you need to win the campaign, you could decide with your gaming group on a completely different way to win the campaign – the victor could be the first player to defeat every other player in the campaign, or the first to amass an army of ten or more units.

Essentially, you should feel free to use these rules in whichever way you and your gaming group agree is best. Your path to glory is limitless!

CHAMPION REWARDS TABLE

As your champion progresses along the Path to Glory, they may be gifted with great rewards by their dark patron… if they are deemed worthy.

2D6 Reward

2 What the Gods Give…: Your champion has offended their patron and is punished by being condemned to spawndom. Lose D3 Glory Points (to a minimum of 0), and remove your champion and all rewards they have gained from this table from your warband roster. If your warband has another **HERO**, that model now takes charge and becomes your new champion (if you do not have any **HEROES**, immediately generate one from the hero followers table to become your new champion). Write down your new champion's name on your warband roster ready for the next battle. Of course, your former champion may still have their uses – if your champion was a **MORTAL** you may immediately add a Chaos Spawn to your warband as a follower.

3 Cycle of Life: Roll a dice for your champion in each of your hero phases. On a 1 the champion immediately suffers 1 mortal wound. On a 4+ you can heal D3 wounds that have been allocated to the champion.

4 Poisonous Blood: Roll a dice after any wounds are inflicted upon your champion. On a 2+ one enemy unit within 1" of your champion suffers 1 mortal wound. If several enemy units are within range, randomly determine which one suffers the mortal wound.

5 Ensorcelled Weapon: Pick one of your champion's weapons (it cannot be a weapon used by a mount if they have one). The Rend characteristic of the weapon is improved by 1 (for example, Rend -1 becomes Rend -2).

6 Oppressive Stench: Subtract 1 from hit rolls for attacks that target your champion in the combat phase.

7 Patronage of Nurgle (Lesser Reward): Your champion gains a reward generated from the lesser reward of Nurgle table on the next page.

8 Patronage of Nurgle (Greater Reward): Your champion gains a reward generated from the greater reward of Nurgle table on the next page.

9 Patronage of Nurgle (Exalted Reward): Your champion gains a reward generated from the exalted reward of Nurgle table on the next page.

10 Daemonic Armour: You can re-roll failed save rolls for your champion.

11 Blubbery Resilience: Roll a dice each time you allocate a wound or mortal wound to your champion. On a 6+ the wound is negated.

12 Twice-blessed Champion: Roll twice on this table and apply both results. Re-roll duplicates and further rolls of 2 or 12.

PATRONAGE OF NURGLE TABLES

If you roll a Patronage of Nurgle result on the champion rewards table, generate a reward from the appropriate table below that matches the extent of Nurgle's favour.

LESSER REWARD

D3	Reward
1	**Putrid Vomit:** Once per game, in your shooting phase, pick an enemy unit within 3" of your champion. Roll a dice for each model in the unit you picked that is within 3" of your champion. For each roll of 5 or 6 the unit suffers 1 mortal wound.
2	**Repellent Smell:** Subtract 2 from any charge rolls made for units attempting to charge your champion.
3	**Inimical Touch:** You can re-roll wound rolls of 1 for your champion.

GREATER REWARD

D3	Reward
1	**Reaping Strikes:** Each time you make a hit roll of 6+ for your champion in the combat phase, they can immediately make one additional attack with the same weapon. Any bonus attacks made in this manner can themselves generate additional attacks.
2	**Bulky Onslaught:** You can re-roll failed wound rolls for your champion in a turn in which they charged.
3	**Baleful Virulence:** Add 1 to the Damage characteristic of one of your champion's melee weapons.

EXALTED REWARD

D3	Reward
1	**Infectious Joviality:** Your units do not need to take battleshock tests if they are within 7" of your champion.
2	**Fly Swarm:** Once per battle, at the start of a combat phase, pick an enemy unit within 7" of your champion. Subtract 1 from any hit rolls made for models in that unit until the end of the phase.
3	**Boon of Regeneration:** Once per battle, in your hero phase, your champion can call upon Nurgle's favour. You can heal D3 wounds that have been allocated to your champion.

SEEDS OF CORRUPTION

HOW TO USE BATTLEPLANS

The following battleplan enables you to fight a battle that epitomises the way the Maggotkin wage war. It should be fought using all of the *Warhammer Age of Sigmar* rules unless specifically indicated otherwise. The battleplan includes a map reflecting the landscape on which the battle is fought. The map is for a battlefield that is 6 feet by 4 feet in size, but you can use a smaller or larger area if you wish.

Nurgle wishes to see rot and contagion bloom across the Mortal Realms, drowning the bastions of his enemies in a tide of putrid filth. Summoning forth the festering vegetation of the Plague God's garden, his ebullient disciples spread his generous blessings far and wide.

THE ARMIES

One player commands a Maggotkin army and their opponent commands the defenders of the realm the Maggotkin are invading. In addition to the armies, you will need at least three Feculent Gnarlmaws.

MAGGOTKIN PLAYER'S OBJECTIVES

Grandfather Nurgle has sent you to these lands, for he wishes to add them to the domains that thrive under his munificent rule. Subdue any defenders, using their corpses as the mulch that will bring forth the Garden of Nurgle.

DEFENDER'S OBJECTIVES

One of Nurgle's armies is approaching the land you hold dear, intent on turning it into a vile, disease-ridden parody of its current form. They must be stopped and driven back at all costs, before the rot that they bring can take hold.

THE BATTLEFIELD

The battlefield represents a fertile hinterland that Nurgle has demanded be brought under his control so that it can be blessed with the many gifts he can bestow. Players can choose to set up scenery as described on the *Warhammer Age of Sigmar* rules sheet. Any terrain features should be set up more than 6" from any cessnodes (see right). Do not set up any Feculent Gnarlmaws on the battlefield before the battle begins (they may appear during the battle, as described below).

CESSNODES

Located in the defender's territory are three cessnodes: locations that are ripe to be corrupted by Nurgle's blessings, and from which can spring forth the first Feculent Gnarlmaws that will form the basis of a new patch of Nurgle's garden. The position of each of the three cessnodes is shown on the deployment map with a fly symbol; you may wish to note their location with suitable marker.

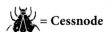 = **Cessnode**

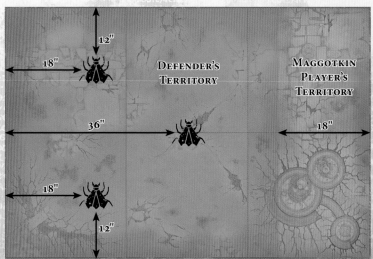

SET-UP

The defender sets up all their units first, anywhere wholly within their territory that is more than 9" from the Maggotkin player's territory (see map). The Maggotkin player sets up second, anywhere wholly within their territory. Do not set up any Feculent Gnarlmaws on the battlefield before the battle begins (they may appear during the battle, as described below).

FIRST TURN

The Maggotkin player takes the first turn in the first battle round.

BRINGING ON THE ROT

The Maggotkin player can change a cessnode into rotnode by summoning a Feculent Gnarlmaw (pg 61) and setting it up on the cessnode's location.

VICTORY

Do not use any of the victory conditions from the *Warhammer Age of Sigmar* rules sheet. Instead, the Maggotkin player immediately wins a **major victory** if all three cessnodes are converted into rotnodes. Otherwise the battle lasts for five battle rounds.

If, at the end of the fifth battle round, the Maggotkin player has only converted up to one cessnode into a rotnode, the defender wins a **major victory**. In any other circumstances, each player calculates a victory score by adding up the Wounds characteristics of all the models that have been slain in the opposing army. The player with the higher score can claim a **minor victory**.

WARSCROLLS

The warriors and creatures that battle in the Mortal Realms are incredibly diverse, and to represent this, every model has a warscroll that lists the characteristics, weapons and abilities that apply to it.

Every Citadel Miniature in the Warhammer range has its own warscroll, which provides you with all of the information needed to use that model in a game of *Warhammer Age of Sigmar*. More information about what a warscroll contains, along with a number of hints and tips for their use, can be found on the page opposite.

In addition, you can organise the units in your army into a special type of formation by using a warscroll battalion. Doing so will give you access to additional abilities that can be used by the units in the battalion.

When you are setting up, you can set up all of the units in a warscroll battalion instead of setting up a single unit. Alternatively, you can set up some of the units from a warscroll battalion, and set up any remaining units individually later on, or you can set up all of the units individually.

Usually, a unit can only belong to one battalion, and so can only benefit from a single set of battalion abilities. However, some very large battalions include other, smaller battalions, and in this case it is possible for a unit to benefit from the abilities of two different battalions at the same time.

The key below explains what you will find on a warscroll battalion.

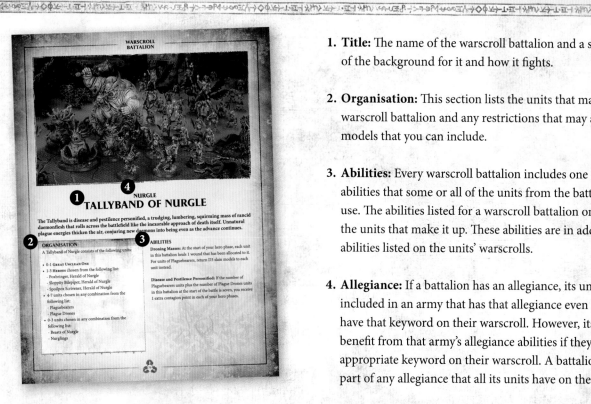

1. **Title:** The name of the warscroll battalion and a short overview of the background for it and how it fights.

2. **Organisation:** This section lists the units that make up the warscroll battalion and any restrictions that may apply to the models that you can include.

3. **Abilities:** Every warscroll battalion includes one or more abilities that some or all of the units from the battalion can use. The abilities listed for a warscroll battalion only apply to the units that make it up. These abilities are in addition to the abilities listed on the units' warscrolls.

4. **Allegiance:** If a battalion has an allegiance, its units can be included in an army that has that allegiance even if they do not have that keyword on their warscroll. However, its units only benefit from that army's allegiance abilities if they have the appropriate keyword on their warscroll. A battalion can still be part of any allegiance that all its units have on their warscrolls.

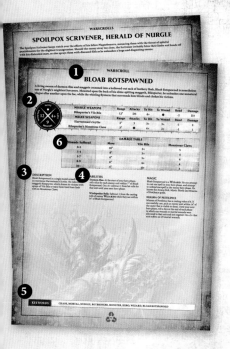

1. **Title:** The name of the model that the warscroll describes.

2. **Characteristics:** This set of characteristics tells you how fast, powerful and brave the model is, and how effective its weapons are.

3. **Description:** The description tells you what weapons the model can be armed with, and what upgrades (if any) it can be given. It will also tell you if the model is fielded on its own, or as part of a unit. If the model is fielded as part of a unit, then the description will say how many models the unit should have (if you don't have enough models to field a unit, you can still field it with as many as you have available).

4. **Abilities:** Abilities are things that the model can do during a game that are not covered by the standard game rules.

5. **Keywords:** All models have a list of keywords. Sometimes a rule will say that it only applies to models that have a specific keyword.

6. **Damage Table:** Some models have a damage table that is used to determine one or more of the model's characteristics. Look up the number of wounds the model has suffered to find the value of the characteristic in question.

Modifiers: Many warscrolls include modifiers that can affect characteristics. For example, a rule might add 1 to the Move characteristic of a model, or subtract 1 from the result of a hit roll. Modifiers are cumulative.

Random Values: Sometimes, the Move or weapon characteristics on a warscroll will have random values. For example, the Move characteristic for a model might be 2D6 (two dice rolls added together), whereas the Attacks characteristic of a weapon might be D6.

When a unit with a random Move characteristic is selected to move in the movement phase, roll the indicated number of dice. The total of the dice rolled is the Move characteristic for all models in the unit for the duration of that phase.

Generate any random values for a weapon (except Damage) each time it is chosen as the weapon for an attack. Roll once and apply the result to all such weapons being used in the attack. The result applies for the rest of that phase. For Damage, generate a value for each weapon that inflicts damage.

When to Use Abilities: Abilities that are used at the start of a phase must be carried out before any other actions. By the same token, abilities used at the end of the phase are carried out after all normal activities for the phase are complete.

If you can use several abilities at the same time, you can decide in which order they are used. If both players can carry out abilities at the same time, the player whose turn is taking place uses their abilities first.

Save of '-': Some models have a Save of '-'. This means that they automatically fail all save rolls (do not make the roll, even if modifiers apply).

Keywords: Keywords are sometimes linked to (or tagged) by a rule. For example, a rule might say that it applies to 'all NURGLE models'. This means that it would apply to models that have the NURGLE keyword on their warscroll.

Minimum Range: Some weapons have a minimum range. For example 6"-48". The weapon cannot shoot at an enemy unit that is within the minimum range.

Weapons: Some models can be armed with two identical weapons. When the model attacks with these weapons, do not double the number of attacks that the weapons make; usually, the model gets an additional ability instead.

NURGLE
THE MUNIFICENT WANDERERS

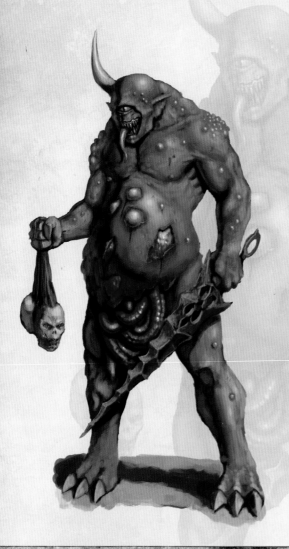

The Munificent Wanderers have been greatly blessed by Nurgle and, following their god's generous example, wish only to share their bountiful foulness with all they meet. As they shamble into battle, their unnatural flesh and rusted blades teem with parasites and plagues that they distribute vigorously. Every claw slash, every bite of rotted fangs, every liquid spray and sword thrust bestows the gifts of Nurgle upon their unfortunate foes.

ORGANISATION

The Munificent Wanderers must contain the following:

- 1 Great Unclean One (Thrombolhox the Giving)
- 2 Tallybands of Nurgle

The Munificent Wanderers may also contain:
- 0-5 additional Tallybands of Nurgle
- Any number of additional **NURGLE DAEMON** units

ABILITIES

Infested with Foul Gifts: In the Rampant Disease stage of the Cycle of Corruption, enemy units that are affected by the Rampant Disease that are within 14" of a unit from this battalion suffer D6 mortal wounds instead of D3 mortal wounds. In addition, if Thrombolhox the Giving is on the battlefield in the Rampant Disease stage of the Cycle of Corruption, then D6 enemy units are affected by the Rampant Disease instead of D3 units.

NURGLE

TALLYBAND OF NURGLE

The Tallyband is disease and pestilence personified, a trudging, lumbering, squirming mass of rancid daemonflesh that rolls across the battlefield like the inexorable approach of death itself. Unnatural plague energies thicken the air, conjuring new daemons into being even as the advance continues.

ORGANISATION

A Tallyband of Nurgle consists of the following units:

- 0-1 GREAT UNCLEAN ONE
- 1-3 HEROES chosen from the following list:
  - Poxbringer, Herald of Nurgle
  - Sloppity Bilepiper, Herald of Nurgle
  - Spoilpox Scrivener, Herald of Nurgle
- 4-7 units chosen in any combination from the following list:
  - Plaguebearers
  - Plague Drones
- 0-3 units chosen in any combination from the following list:
  - Beasts of Nurgle
  - Nurglings

ABILITIES

Droning Masses: At the start of your hero phase, each unit in this battalion heals 1 wound that has been allocated to it. For units of Plaguebearers, return D3 slain models to each unit instead.

Disease and Pestilence Personified: If the number of Plaguebearers units plus the number of Plague Drones units in this battalion at the start of the battle is seven, you receive 1 extra contagion point in each of your hero phases.

NURGLE
THRICEFOLD BEFOULMENT

The ground shakes beneath the tread of this revolting trio as they lumber to war. The Great Unclean Ones of the Thricefold Befoulment are the living embodiment of Nurgle's tri-lobed sigil writ vast in rotting flesh and pulsating power, and nothing pure or untainted can stand before their might.

ORGANISATION

A Thricefold Befoulment consists of the following units:

- 3 Great Unclean Ones

ABILITIES

Hungry for the Plague God's Praise: Re-roll hit rolls of 1 for models from this battalion while they are within 14" of another model from this battalion. In addition, re-roll wound rolls of 1 for models from this battalion while they are within 14" of two other models from this battalion.

Plague Storm of Nurgle: If a model from this battalion successfully casts the Plague Wind spell when it is within 7" of another model from this battalion, then the number of mortal wounds inflicted by the spell is increased from D3 to 2D3. If the caster is within 7" of two other models from this battalion, then the number of mortal wounds inflicted by the spell is increased to 3D3 instead.

NURGLE
NURGLE'S MENAGERIE

From the festering depths of Nurgle's realm, his filthsome pretties spill forth. Loping on bloated limbs or ploughing through the air on buzzing wings, these abominations obey the croaked commands of Horticulous Slimux, burying their victims in an avalanche of rancid flesh and lethal ebullience.

ORGANISATION

Nurgle's Menagerie consists of the following units:

- Horticulous Slimux
- 3 units of Beasts of Nurgle
- Up to 3 units chosen in any combination from the following list:
  - Plague Drones
  - Beasts of Nurgle
  - Nurglings

ABILITIES

Assistant Gardeners: Horticulous Slimux can use his Cultivating the Garden of Nurgle ability in each of your hero phases instead of only once per battle. In addition, when he does so, the Feculent Gnarlmaw can be set up within 3" of any unit from this battalion instead of being set up within 3" of Horticulous Slimux.

Utterly Revolting Horde: Subtract 1 from the Bravery characteristic of enemy units while they are within 14" of 7 or more models from this battalion.

NURGLE
THE BLESSED SONS

Long and droning are the prideful chants of the Blessed Sons as they enumerate the glories they have won in Nurgle's name. Even as they butcher their foes, they gloat and chortle, goading their enemies in their arrogance and pouring scorn upon their cleanliness and unsavoury good health. For all their hoarse braggadocio, the Blessed Sons are ferociously dangerous warriors, worthy bearers of Nurgle's rancid gifts.

ORGANISATION

The Blessed Sons must contain the following:

- 1 Plague Cyst that includes a Sorcerer, Harbinger of Decay and at least 4 units of Putrid Blightkings

The Blessed Sons may also contain:
- 0-6 additional warscroll battalions chosen from the following list:
  - Plague Cyst
  - Blight Cyst
  - Affliction Cyst
- Any number of additional ROTBRINGER units

ABILITIES

Swollen with Pride: Units in this battalion do not have to take battleshock tests while they have 7 or more models.

Blessed Blightplate: Re-roll save rolls of 1 for models in this battalion.

NURGLE
PLAGUE CYST

The warriors of a Plague Cyst are as direct and aggressive as their lord. They view their enemies as little more than living sacks of meat and fluids, waiting to be split open and strewn as plague-fertiliser across the battlefields of the Mortal Realms.

ORGANISATION

A Plague Cyst consists of the following units:

- 1 Lord of Plagues
- 3-6 units of Putrid Blightkings
- 0-1 Sorcerer
- 0-1 Harbinger of Decay

ABILITIES

Master of Slaughter: Re-roll all failed hit rolls for units from this battalion that are affected by the Wanton Slaughter ability of this battalion's Lord of Plagues, instead of only re-rolling hit rolls of 1.

Horribly Contagious: In your hero phase, roll a dice for each enemy unit within 3" of any units from this battalion. On a 6+ the unit being rolled for suffers D3 mortal wounds.

NURGLE
BLIGHT CYST

To stand against the Blight Cyst is to be beset by virulent foulness at every turn. Hails of filth-filled death's heads rain down upon the enemy and swarms of biting flies envelop them in a blinding, choking mass, before the pox-ridden servants of Nurgle hack their way through the diseased survivors.

ORGANISATION

A Blight Cyst consists of the following units:

- 1 Lord of Blights
- 3-6 units of Putrid Blightkings
- 0-1 Sorcerer
- 0-1 Harbinger of Decay

ABILITIES

Endless Bounty: The Munificent Bounty ability of this battalion's Lord of Blights affects all units from this battalion that are within 3" of him at the start of your shooting phase, instead of only one unit.

Supremely Blighted Weapons: The Blighted Weapons used by the Putrid Blightkings in this battalion have a Rend characteristic of '-1'.

Blights on the Landscape: In the combat phase, enemy units do not receive any benefits for being in cover against attacks made by this battalion.

NURGLE
AFFLICTION CYST

The air fills with the thunderous drone of membranous wings as the warriors of the Affliction Cyst ride their bloated Rot Flies into battle. Enemies scatter in panic as Pusgoyle Blightlords plunge down from on high, their dark shadows heralding disease and death.

ORGANISATION

An Affliction Cyst consists of the following units:

- 1 Lord of Afflictions
- 3-6 units of Pusgoyle Blightlords

ABILITIES

The Droning Sky: Instead of setting up a unit from this battalion on the battlefield, you can place it to one side and say that it is set up hovering in the skies. You can do this with as many units from the battalion as you wish. At the end of your first movement phase, set up each of these units more than 9" from any enemy models.

Diseased Onslaught: If the Lord of Afflictions from this battalion uses his Spearhead of Contagion command ability, it affects all units from this battalion that are within 14" of him, instead of only one unit.

ROTIGUS

Brandishing his gnarlrod to the skies, Rotigus Rainfather calls down the inundating Deluge of Nurgle. From the fanged maws that split his flesh he vomits thundering streams of brackish filth, drowning the enemy in his plentiful gifts even as he mires the battlefield in cloying mud and diseased, stinking floods of slime.

MELEE WEAPONS	Range	Attacks	To Hit	To Wound	Rend	Damage
Gnarlrod	3"	5	✸	3+	-1	2
Fanged Maw	1"	D3	3+	✸	-2	2
Host of Nurglings	1"	3	5+	5+	-	1

DAMAGE TABLE			
Wounds Allocated	Gnarlrod	Fanged Maw	Deluge of Nurgle
0-3	2+	2+	4+
4-6	3+	2+	5+
7-9	3+	3+	5+
10-12	4+	3+	6+
13+	4+	4+	6+

DESCRIPTION
Rotigus is a single model. He carries a Gnarlrod that can be used to strike at enemies that are nearby. A Host of Nurglings caper about his feet, attacking with their razor-sharp teeth, while the Fanged Maw in his belly snaps and bites at the foe.

ABILITIES
Blubber and Bile: Roll a dice each time you allocate a wound or mortal wound to Rotigus. On a 5+ the wound is negated. In addition, if the roll is 6+ and it is the combat phase, the attacking unit suffers 1 mortal wound after all of its attacks have been made.

Corpulent Mass: In your hero phase, you can heal D3 wounds that have been allocated to Rotigus.

Mountain of Loathsome Flesh: Roll a dice for each enemy unit that is within 1" of Rotigus after he completes a charge move. On a 4+ the enemy unit suffers D3 mortal wounds.

Streams of Brackish Filth: In your hero phase, roll a dice for each enemy unit that is within 6" of Rotigus. On a 4+ the enemy unit suffers D3 mortal wounds. Enemy units that can fly suffer D3 mortal wounds on a 6+ instead of a 4+.

MAGIC
Rotigus is a **WIZARD**. He can attempt to cast two spells in your hero phase, and attempt to unbind two spells in the enemy hero phase. He knows the Arcane Bolt, Mystic Shield and Deluge of Nurgle spells.

DELUGE OF NURGLE
Deluge of Nurgle has a casting value of 7. If successfully cast, roll 7 dice. For each roll that equals or beats the Deluge of Nurgle value shown on the damage table above, you can pick an enemy unit that is visible to the caster. That unit suffers D3 mortal wounds. If this spell affects more than one enemy unit, you must pick a different enemy unit to suffer each set of D3 mortal wounds.

KEYWORDS CHAOS, DAEMON, NURGLE, MONSTER, HERO, WIZARD, GREAT UNCLEAN ONE, ROTIGUS

GREAT UNCLEAN ONE

The mightiest of Nurgle's daemons, the Great Unclean Ones are immensely resilient and frighteningly strong. Able to barge down fortress gates and crush monstrous beasts with their sheer bulk, Great Unclean Ones exude disease and decay as they smash their way through the foe. Meanwhile, their grasp of high strategy and their magical talents make them formidable generals.

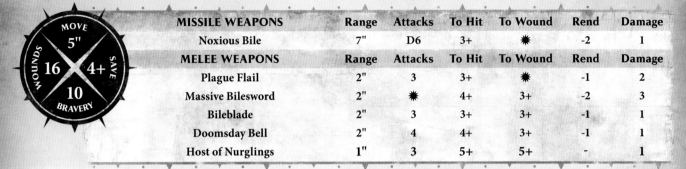

MISSILE WEAPONS	Range	Attacks	To Hit	To Wound	Rend	Damage
Noxious Bile	7"	D6	3+	✷	-2	1
MELEE WEAPONS	**Range**	**Attacks**	**To Hit**	**To Wound**	**Rend**	**Damage**
Plague Flail	2"	3	3+	✷	-1	2
Massive Bilesword	2"	✷	4+	3+	-2	3
Bileblade	2"	3	3+	3+	-1	1
Doomsday Bell	2"	4	4+	3+	-1	1
Host of Nurglings	1"	3	5+	5+	-	1

MOVE 5"
WOUNDS 16
SAVE 4+
BRAVERY 10

DAMAGE TABLE			
Wounds Allocated	Noxious Bile	Plague Flail	Massive Bilesword
0-3	2+	2+	3
4-6	3+	3+	3
7-9	3+	3+	2
10-12	4+	4+	2
13+	5+	4+	1

DESCRIPTION
A Great Unclean One is a single model. It carries a large Plague Flail or Bileblade in one hand, and a Massive Bilesword or Doomsday Bell in the other, and can vomit forth streams of Noxious Bile. A Host of Nurglings caper about the Great Unclean One's feet, attacking with their razor-sharp teeth.

ABILITIES
Blubber and Bile: Roll a dice each time you allocate a wound or mortal wound to this model. On a 5+ the wound is negated. In addition, if the roll is 6+ and it is the combat phase, the attacking unit suffers 1 mortal wound after all of its attacks have been made.

Corpulent Mass: In your hero phase, you can heal D3 wounds that have been allocated to this model.

Mountain of Loathsome Flesh: Roll a dice for each enemy unit that is within 1" of this model after this model completes a charge move. On a 4+ the enemy unit suffers D3 mortal wounds.

Putrid Offering: If this model has a Bileblade and attempts to cast or unbind a spell, you can say that it is using the Bileblade to hook out a portion of its own rotting guts as an offering to Nurgle. If you do so, this model immediately suffers 1 mortal wound (which cannot be negated), but you can then add 1 to the casting or unbinding roll.

Reverberating Summons: If a **Nurgle** unit begins its movement phase within 7" of any models with a Doomsday Bell, add 3 to its Move characteristic until the end of the phase.

COMMAND ABILITY
Grandfather's Joy: You can use this command ability in your hero phase. If you do, pick a friendly **Nurgle Daemon** unit within 21" of this model. Add 1 to the Attacks characteristic of all melee weapons used by that unit until your next hero phase.

MAGIC
A Great Unclean One is a **Wizard**. It can attempt to cast two spells in your hero phase, and attempt to unbind two spells in the enemy hero phase. It knows the Arcane Bolt, Mystic Shield and Plague Wind spells.

PLAGUE WIND
Plague Wind has a casting value of 7. If successfully cast, pick a point on the battlefield within 14" of the caster and draw an imaginary straight line between it and the closest part of the caster. Each unit (friend or foe) crossed by the centre of the line suffers D3 mortal wounds. Units with the **Nurgle** keyword are instead invigorated by the Plague Wind; if it passes over them, heal D3 wounds that have been allocated to the unit.

KEYWORDS	CHAOS, DAEMON, NURGLE, MONSTER, HERO, WIZARD, GREAT UNCLEAN ONE

POXBRINGER, HERALD OF NURGLE

These powerful daemonic heroes lead their brother Plaguebearers into battle, and ensure that the orders of the Great Unclean Ones are followed to the letter. They are potent warriors, whose baleswords can kill with a single cut, whose rotted bodies are all but impervious to harm, and whose diseased magics can tear the heart from the foe or bolster their own disgusting foot soldiers.

MELEE WEAPONS	Range	Attacks	To Hit	To Wound	Rend	Damage
Balesword	1"	3	3+	3+	-1	D3

MOVE 4"
WOUNDS 5
SAVE 4+
BRAVERY 10

DESCRIPTION
A Poxbringer is a single model. It wields a repulsive Balesword that weeps vile toxins.

ABILITIES
Disgustingly Resilient: Roll a dice each time you allocate a wound or mortal wound to this model. On a 5+ the wound is negated.

In Death There is Life: At the start of your hero phase, if any models (friend or foe) were slain in the last turn, you can heal 1 wound allocated to a friendly **Nurgle Daemon** unit within 7" of this model.

MAGIC
A Poxbringer is a **Wizard**. It can attempt to cast one spell in your hero phase, and attempt to unbind one spell in the enemy hero phase. It knows the Arcane Bolt, Mystic Shield and Eruptive Infestation spells.

ERUPTIVE INFESTATION
Eruptive Infestation has a casting value of 6. If successfully cast, pick an enemy unit that is within 7" of a friendly Plaguebearers unit and visible to the caster. That unit suffers D3 mortal wounds.

KEYWORDS CHAOS, DAEMON, PLAGUEBEARER, NURGLE, HERO, POXBRINGER, HERALD OF NURGLE

EPIDEMIUS, TALLYMAN OF NURGLE

Sat high upon his mouldering palanquin, borne aloft by a suppurating mound of subservient Nurglings, Epidemius casts his single eye across the battlefield with jaded contempt. His bone quill scratches upon cured-flesh parchment, enumerating the endless tally of Nurgle's diseases, and as the count rises ever higher so the Plague God's minions become ever more empowered.

MELEE WEAPONS	Range	Attacks	To Hit	To Wound	Rend	Damage
Balesword	1"	3	3+	3+	-1	D3
Tiny Razor-sharp Teeth	1"	5	5+	5+	-	1

MOVE 4"
WOUNDS 7
SAVE 4+
BRAVERY 10

DESCRIPTION
Epidemius is a single model. He is armed with a malignant Balesword and is carried into battle atop his palanquin by a horde of Nurglings, which attack nearby enemies with their Tiny Razor-sharp Teeth.

ABILITIES
Disgustingly Resilient: Roll a dice each time you allocate a wound or mortal wound to this model. On a 5+ the wound is negated.

Nurgle's Tallyman: Keep a tally of the number of enemy models that have been slain by friendly **Nurgle** units during the battle. At the start of your hero phase, consult the following table to see what benefits are bestowed upon friendly **Nurgle** units:

Models Slain	Effect
0-6	No effect.
7-13	Re-roll wound rolls of 1.
14-20	Re-roll hit rolls of 1.
21+	Receive 1 extra contagion point in each of your hero phases.

These bonuses are cumulative and last for the rest of the battle, but end if Epidemius is slain.

KEYWORDS CHAOS, DAEMON, PLAGUEBEARER, NURGLE, HERO, EPIDEMIUS, TALLYMAN OF NURGLE

SPOILPOX SCRIVENER, HERALD OF NURGLE

The Spoilpox Scrivener keeps watch over the efforts of his fellow Plaguebearers, menacing them with the threat of spiteful punishments for the slightest transgression. Should the enemy stray too close, the Scrivener irritably bites their limbs and heads off with his distended maw, or else sprays them with diseased filth as he unleashes a huge and disgusting sneeze.

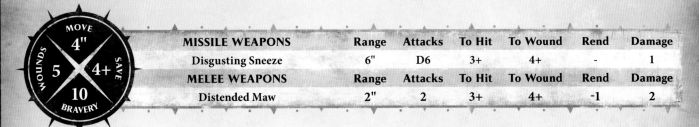

MISSILE WEAPONS	Range	Attacks	To Hit	To Wound	Rend	Damage
Disgusting Sneeze	6"	D6	3+	4+	-	1
MELEE WEAPONS	Range	Attacks	To Hit	To Wound	Rend	Damage
Distended Maw	2"	2	3+	4+	-1	2

MOVE 4"
WOUNDS 5
SAVE 4+
BRAVERY 10

DESCRIPTION
A Spoilpox Scrivener is a single model. It sprays corrosive filth over the enemy with its Disgusting Sneezes, and bites any foe that strays too close with its horrible Distended Maw.

ABILITIES
Disgustingly Resilient: Roll a dice each time you allocate a wound or mortal wound to this model. On a 5+ the wound is negated.

Keep Counting, I'm Watching You: Re-roll dice rolls of 1 when making charge rolls for friendly Plaguebearers units while they are within 7" of this model. In addition, re-roll hit rolls of 1 for friendly Plaguebearers units while they are within 7" of this model.

KEYWORDS | CHAOS, DAEMON, PLAGUEBEARER, NURGLE, HERO, SPOILPOX SCRIVENER, HERALD OF NURGLE

SLOPPITY BILEPIPER, HERALD OF NURGLE

Sloppity Bilepipers caper through the ranks of the Plague Legions as they advance. Infected with a plague of mirth, they prance and quip, entertaining Nurgle's daemons even as they cause the enemy to literally die laughing. With a rasp on their gutpipes they can inspire their allies with unnatural glee, while a single blow from their marotter is enough to reduce most foes to a grinning corpse.

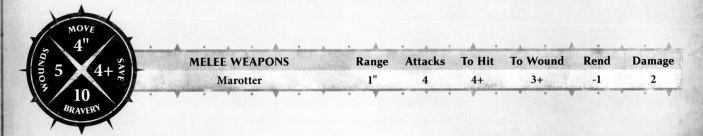

MELEE WEAPONS	Range	Attacks	To Hit	To Wound	Rend	Damage
Marotter	1"	4	4+	3+	-1	2

MOVE 4"
WOUNDS 5
SAVE 4+
BRAVERY 10

DESCRIPTION
A Sloppity Bilepiper is a single model. It is armed with a Marotter.

ABILITIES
Disgustingly Resilient: Roll a dice each time you allocate a wound or mortal wound to this model. On a 5+ the wound is negated.

Disease of Mirth: Add 1 to the Bravery characteristic of friendly **NURGLE DAEMON** units while they are within 7" of any Sloppity Bilepipers. In addition, subtract 1 from the Bravery characteristics of enemy units while they are within 7" of any Sloppity Bilepipers.

Jolly Gutpipes: Re-roll failed charge rolls and hit rolls of 1 for friendly Nurglings and **GREAT UNCLEAN ONE** units while they are within 7" of any Sloppity Bilepipers.

KEYWORDS | CHAOS, DAEMON, PLAGUEBEARER, NURGLE, HERO, SLOPPITY BILEPIPER, HERALD OF NURGLE

HORTICULOUS SLIMUX

Horticulous Slimux rides into battle perched upon the shell of his lumbering daemonic steed, Mulch. As Nurgle's head gardener, he has the power to seed the Garden of Nurgle into the fabric of reality, churning the ground with his Gruntleplough to summon it forth. Surrounded by packs of Beasts of Nurgle and wielding his lethal lopping shears, Horticulous is a being to be greatly feared.

MELEE WEAPONS	Range	Attacks	To Hit	To Wound	Rend	Damage
Lopping Shears	1"	3	3+	3+	-1	D3
Mulch's Slime-encrusted Jaws	1"	D3	3+	3+	-2	2

DESCRIPTION

Horticulous Slimux is a single model. He is armed with a huge pair of Lopping Shears that he uses to snip his enemies in half, and rides upon the back of a molluscoid daemon-beast called Mulch that snaps at the foe with its Slime-encrusted Jaws.

ABILITIES

Disgustingly Resilient: Roll a dice each time you allocate a wound or mortal wound to this model. On a 5+ the wound is negated.

Acidic Slime Trail: Roll a dice for each enemy unit that is within 3" of this model immediately before this model makes a retreat move. On a 4+ that enemy unit suffers D3 mortal wounds.

Beast Handler: Re-roll failed charge rolls and hit rolls of 1 for friendly Beasts of Nurgle units while they are within 7" of Horticulous Slimux.

In Death There is Life: At the start of your hero phase, if any models (friend or foe) were slain in the last turn, you can heal 1 wound allocated to a friendly **Nurgle Daemon** unit within 7" of Horticulous Slimux.

Cultivating the Garden of Nurgle: Once during the battle, at the start of your hero phase, you can set up a Feculent Gnarlmaw within 3" of Horticulous Slimux and more than 1" away from any other model or terrain feature.

KEYWORDS	CHAOS, DAEMON, PLAGUEBEARER, NURGLE, HERO, HORTICULOUS SLIMUX

PLAGUEBEARERS

Plaguebearers trudge to battle amidst the drone of flies' wings and endless counting. These corpse-like daemons tally the diseases unleashed by Nurgle upon the Mortal Realms, and as they do so they stab and hack at their enemies with filth-ridden plagueswords. Relentless and resilient in equal measure, Plaguebearers overwhelm their victims as surely as a terminal sickness.

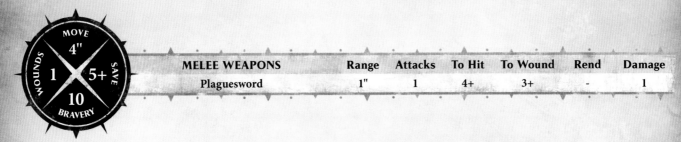

MOVE 4"
SAVE 5+
BRAVERY 10
WOUNDS 1

MELEE WEAPONS	Range	Attacks	To Hit	To Wound	Rend	Damage
Plaguesword	1"	1	4+	3+	-	1

DESCRIPTION
A unit of Plaguebearers has 10 or more models. They are armed with vile Plagueswords.

PLAGUERIDDEN
The leader of this unit is a Plagueridden. Add 1 to the Attacks characteristic of a Plagueridden's Plaguesword.

ICON BEARER
Models in this unit can be Icon Bearers. If the unmodified roll is a 1 when making a battleshock test for a unit that includes any Icon Bearers, no models from the unit flee. Instead, D6 Plaguebearer models are added to the unit.

PIPERS
Models in this unit can be Pipers. Re-roll battleshock rolls of 1 for enemy units while they are within 6" of any Pipers.

ABILITIES
Disgustingly Resilient: Roll a dice each time you allocate a wound or mortal wound to a model in this unit. On a 5+ the wound is negated.

Cloud of Flies: Subtract 1 from the hit rolls of attacks that target this unit in the shooting phase. If this unit contains 20 or more models, subtract 2 from the hit rolls of attacks that target this unit in the shooting phase, and 1 from the hit rolls of attacks that target this unit in the combat phase instead.

Locus of Fecundity: Re-roll save rolls of 1 for this unit while it is within 7" of a friendly **NURGLE DAEMON HERO**.

KEYWORDS	CHAOS, DAEMON, PLAGUEBEARER, NURGLE, PLAGUEBEARERS

PLAGUE DRONES

Amongst the swiftest and most dangerous of Nurgle's followers, Plague Drones are high-ranking Plaguebearers who ride to war astride huge and malevolent Rot Flies. These daemonic airborne mounts attack the foe with stingers, proboscises, foul mouthparts and chitinous limbs, while their riders hurl death's heads into the enemy lines that explode in showers of infectious filth.

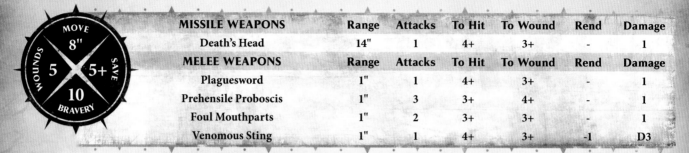

MISSILE WEAPONS	Range	Attacks	To Hit	To Wound	Rend	Damage
Death's Head	14"	1	4+	3+	-	1
MELEE WEAPONS	Range	Attacks	To Hit	To Wound	Rend	Damage
Plaguesword	1"	1	4+	3+	-	1
Prehensile Proboscis	1"	3	3+	4+	-	1
Foul Mouthparts	1"	2	3+	3+	-	1
Venomous Sting	1"	1	4+	3+	-1	D3

Stats circle: MOVE 8", WOUNDS 5, SAVE 5+, BRAVERY 10

DESCRIPTION
A unit of Plague Drones has 3 or more models. The Rot Flies stab the enemy with Venomous Stings, and either lash at the foe with a Prehensile Proboscis or bite with Foul Mouthparts. Their Plaguebearer riders swing Plagueswords and throw virulent Death's Heads.

FLY
Plague Drones can fly.

PLAGUEBRINGER
The leader of this unit is a Plaguebringer. Add 1 to the Attacks characteristic of a Plaguebringer's Plaguesword.

ICON BEARER
Models in this unit can be Icon Bearers. If the unmodified roll is a 1 when making a battleshock test for a unit that includes any Icon Bearers, no models from the unit flee. Instead, 1 Plague Drone model is added to the unit.

BELL TOLLERS
Models in this unit can be Bell Tollers. Re-roll battleshock rolls of 1 for enemy units while they are within 6" of any Bell Tollers.

ABILITIES
Disgustingly Resilient: Roll a dice each time you allocate a wound or mortal wound to a model in this unit. On a 5+ the wound is negated.

Locus of Contagion: Add 1 to the Attacks characteristics of this unit's weapons while it is within 7" of a friendly **NURGLE DAEMON HERO**.

KEYWORDS	CHAOS, DAEMON, PLAGUEBEARER, NURGLE, PLAGUE DRONES

BEASTS OF NURGLE

As stupid as they are enthusiastic, Beasts of Nurgle bound into battle with burbling bellows of joy. Huge, slug-like abominations with fanged maws and diseased tentacles, their flabby bodies exude a paralytic slime that renders their victims helpless. The Beasts of Nurgle gleefully rip and crush their luckless playmates until their joy proves lethal, before bounding off in search of new victims.

MELEE WEAPONS	Range	Attacks	To Hit	To Wound	Rend	Damage
Claws and Tentacles	1"	D6	4+	3+	-	1
Slobbering Tongue	2"	1	3+	3+	-	D3

DESCRIPTION
A unit of Beasts of Nurgle has any number of models. Beasts of Nurgle unintentionally rend and crush their victims their Claws and Tentacles, and poison them with their Slobbering Tongues.

ABILITIES
Disgustingly Resilient: Roll a dice each time you allocate a wound or mortal wound to this model. On a 5+ the wound is negated.

Acidic Slime Trail: Roll a dice for each enemy unit that is within 3" of this unit immediately before this unit makes a retreat move. On a 4+ that enemy unit suffers D3 mortal wounds.

Attention Seekers: This unit can charge in the same turn in which it ran or retreated.

Locus of Virulence: Add 1 to the Damage characteristics of this unit's weapons while it is within 7" of a friendly **NURGLE DAEMON HERO**.

KEYWORDS	CHAOS, DAEMON, NURGLE, BEASTS OF NURGLE

NURGLINGS

Nurglings are diseased daemon mites, miniature facsimiles of their noisome god that pour across the battlefield in a stinking tide and bury the foe beneath wave after wave of bloated little bodies. Tumbling from the innards of larger daemons or spilling up from sewers and fissures, the diminutive daemons overcome their victims with sheer weight of numbers and infectious foulness.

MELEE WEAPONS	Range	Attacks	To Hit	To Wound	Rend	Damage
Tiny Razor-sharp Teeth	1"	5	5+	5+	-	1

DESCRIPTION
A unit of Nurglings has 3 or more models. Nurglings attack with their Tiny Razor-sharp Teeth.

ABILITIES
Disease-ridden Demise: At the end of the combat phase, roll a dice for each enemy unit that was allocated any wounds caused by a unit of Nurglings in that combat phase. On a 2+ that unit suffers 1 mortal wound.

Endless Swarm: At the end of the battleshock phase, heal any wounds that have been allocated to this unit.

Hidden Infestations: Instead of setting up this unit on the battlefield, you can place it to one side and say that it is set up as a hidden infestation of Nurglings. If you do so, at the end of your first movement phase, set up the unit anywhere on the battlefield so that it is in cover and more than 9" from any enemy models.

KEYWORDS	CHAOS, DAEMON, NURGLE, NURGLINGS

THE GLOTTKIN

Plague-cursed triplets of immense age and power, the Glottkin are Nurgle's greatest mortal champions. Otto the warrior lord and Ethrac the plague sorcerer ride to war upon the lumpen shoulders of their monstrous brother, Ghurk, and together their unnatural power is great enough to drive vast armies into battle and crush all who stand against them.

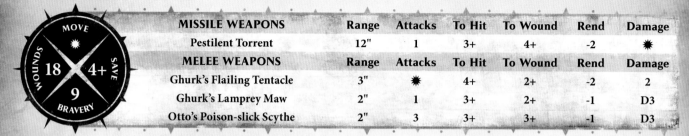

MISSILE WEAPONS	Range	Attacks	To Hit	To Wound	Rend	Damage
Pestilent Torrent	12"	1	3+	4+	-2	✹
MELEE WEAPONS	**Range**	**Attacks**	**To Hit**	**To Wound**	**Rend**	**Damage**
Ghurk's Flailing Tentacle	3"	✹	4+	2+	-2	2
Ghurk's Lamprey Maw	2"	1	3+	2+	-1	D3
Otto's Poison-slick Scythe	2"	3	3+	3+	-1	D3

MOVE ✹ — SAVE 4+ — WOUNDS 18 — BRAVERY 9

DAMAGE TABLE			
Wounds Allocated	Move	Pestilent Torrent	Ghurk's Flailing Tentacle
0-3	8"	2D6	6
4-6	7"	D6	5
7-9	6"	D3	4
10-12	5"	2	3
13+	4"	1	2

DESCRIPTION

The Glottkin are a single model. Ghurk Glott is a heaving mass of flesh, attacking with a Flailing Tentacle and scooping hapless victims into his Lamprey Maw. His brothers Ethrac and Otto ride upon his festering, boil-encrusted shoulders; Ethrac casts foul spells while Otto attacks with his Poison-slick Scythe and unleashes a Pestilent Torrent of corrosive filth from his swollen gut.

ABILITIES

Mountain of Loathsome Flesh: Roll a dice for each enemy unit that is within 1" of this model after this model completes a charge move. On a 4+ the enemy unit suffers D3 mortal wounds.

Blessings of Nurgle: At the start of your hero phase, you can heal D3 wounds that have been allocated to this model.

Horrific Opponent: At the start of the combat phase, roll 2D6 for each enemy unit within 7" of this model. If the roll is greater than that unit's Bravery characteristic, subtract 1 from hit rolls for that unit in that combat phase.

MAGIC

Ethrac Glott is a **WIZARD**. He can attempt to cast two spells in your hero phase, and attempt to unbind one spell in the enemy hero phase. He knows the Arcane Bolt, Mystic Shield and Fleshy Abundance spells.

FLESHY ABUNDANCE

Fleshy Abundance has a casting value of 7. If successfully cast, pick a friendly unit within 14" of the caster that is visible to them. Add 1 to the Wounds characteristic of all models in that unit until your next hero phase. At the start of your next hero phase, the unit's Wounds characteristic is reduced to its original value. Note that this can result in a model that has been allocated wounds being slain.

COMMAND ABILITY

Lords of Nurgle: You can use this command ability in your hero phase. If you do, then until your next hero phase add 1 to the Attacks characteristic of any melee weapons used by friendly **NURGLE** units while they are within 14" of this model.

KEYWORDS	CHAOS, MORTAL, NURGLE, ROTBRINGER, MONSTER, HERO, WIZARD, THE GLOTTKIN

ORGHOTTS DAEMONSPEW

A driven and merciless warlord, Orghotts Daemonspew is half human and half daemon in nature. He rides to battle astride the gangling pox maggoth Whippermaw, wielding his twinned Rotaxes to devastating effect while his steed's envenomed tongue lashes out to throttle and ensnare. Even should the foe injure Orghotts it is they who truly suffer, as corrosive ichor jets from the wound.

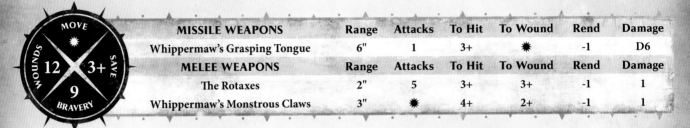

MISSILE WEAPONS	Range	Attacks	To Hit	To Wound	Rend	Damage
Whippermaw's Grasping Tongue	6"	1	3+	✸	-1	D6
MELEE WEAPONS	**Range**	**Attacks**	**To Hit**	**To Wound**	**Rend**	**Damage**
The Rotaxes	2"	5	3+	3+	-1	1
Whippermaw's Monstrous Claws	3"	✸	4+	2+	-1	1

MOVE 12 / 3+ **SAVE** / 9 **BRAVERY** / **WOUNDS**

DAMAGE TABLE			
Wounds Allocated	Move	Grasping Tongue	Monstrous Claws
0-2	10"	2+	5
3-4	8"	3+	4
5-7	6"	4+	4
8-9	6"	5+	4
10+	4"	6+	3

DESCRIPTION

Orghotts Daemonspew is a single model armed with his trusty Rotaxes. He rides his maggoth steed, Whippermaw, which seeks out victims with its Grasping Tongue to drag them into its fang-lined maw, or crushes them with its Monstrous Claws.

ABILITIES

Acid Ichor: Roll a dice each time you allocate a wound to this model in the combat phase (and it is not negated). On a 4+ the attacking unit suffers 1 mortal wound after all of its attacks have been made.

Fury of the Halfblood: Add D3 to the Attacks characteristic of Orghotts Daemonspew's Rotaxes if he made a charge move in the same turn.

The Rotaxes: At the end of the combat phase, roll a dice for each enemy model that was allocated any wounds caused by the Rotaxes in that combat phase and was not slain. On a 4+ that model suffers 1 mortal wound.

COMMAND ABILITY

Fester and Rot: You can use this command ability in your hero phase. If you do, pick a friendly **NURGLE** unit within 14" of Orghotts Daemonspew. Re-roll failed wound rolls for that unit until your next hero phase.

KEYWORDS CHAOS, MORTAL, NURGLE, ROTBRINGER, MONSTER, HERO, ORGHOTTS DAEMONSPEW

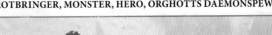

BLOAB ROTSPAWNED

A living swarm of daemon-flies and maggots crammed into a hollowed-out sack of leathery flesh, Bloab Rotspawned is nonetheless one of Nurgle's mightiest Sorcerers. Mounted upon the back of his slime-spitting maggoth, Bilespurter, he unleashes one unnatural plague after another upon the foe, while the whirling flystorm that surrounds him blinds and chokes his victims.

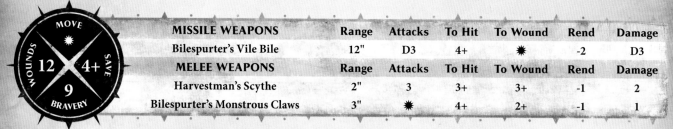

MOVE X **SAVE** 4+
WOUNDS 12
BRAVERY 9

MISSILE WEAPONS	Range	Attacks	To Hit	To Wound	Rend	Damage
Bilespurter's Vile Bile	12"	D3	4+	✷	-2	D3
MELEE WEAPONS	**Range**	**Attacks**	**To Hit**	**To Wound**	**Rend**	**Damage**
Harvestman's Scythe	2"	3	3+	3+	-1	2
Bilespurter's Monstrous Claws	3"	✷	4+	2+	-1	1

DAMAGE TABLE

Wounds Allocated	Move	Vile Bile	Monstrous Claws
0-2	10"	2+	5
3-4	8"	3+	4
5-7	6"	3+	4
8-9	6"	4+	4
10+	4"	4+	3

DESCRIPTION

Bloab Rotspawned is a single model armed with an enormous Harvestman's Scythe. He rides the maggoth Bilespurter, which douses its victims with sprays of Vile Bile or tears them limb from limb with its Monstrous Claws.

ABILITIES

Daemon-flies: At the start of your hero phase, roll a dice for each enemy unit within 7" of Bloab Rotspawned. On a 4+ subtract 1 from hit rolls for that unit until your next hero phase.

Windspeaker Bells: Subtract 1 from the casting rolls of enemy **WIZARDS** while they are within 14" of Bloab Rotspawned.

MAGIC

Bloab Rotspawned is a **WIZARD**. He can attempt to cast one spell in your hero phase, and attempt to unbind one spell in the enemy hero phase. He knows the Arcane Bolt, Mystic Shield and Miasma of Pestilence spells.

MIASMA OF PESTILENCE

Miasma of Pestilence has a casting value of 6. If successfully cast, pick an enemy unit within 14" of the caster that is visible to them. Until your next hero phase, roll a dice at the end of each phase in which any wounds or mortal wounds were allocated to that unit and not negated. On a 2+ that unit suffers D3 mortal wounds.

KEYWORDS | CHAOS, MORTAL, NURGLE, ROTBRINGER, MONSTER, HERO, WIZARD, BLOAB ROTSPAWNED

MORBIDEX TWICEBORN

Morbidex Twiceborn is the chosen mortal champion of the Nurglings. Twisted by the daemon mites' unnatural touch, he has come to resemble them physically, and has gained much of their unnatural resilience. His disgusting maggoth, Tripletongue, is equally hard to hurt, dragging screaming victims into its maw and devouring them even as Morbidex hacks others apart with his huge scythe.

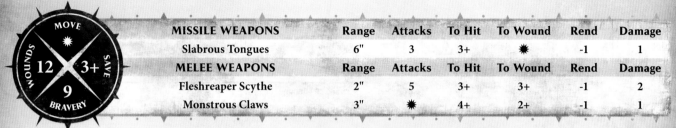

MISSILE WEAPONS	Range	Attacks	To Hit	To Wound	Rend	Damage
Slabrous Tongues	6"	3	3+	✹	-1	1
MELEE WEAPONS	Range	Attacks	To Hit	To Wound	Rend	Damage
Fleshreaper Scythe	2"	5	3+	3+	-1	2
Monstrous Claws	3"	✹	4+	2+	-1	1

Move: ✹ / 10"–4" · Wounds: 12 · Save: 3+ · Bravery: 9

DAMAGE TABLE			
Wounds Allocated	Move	Slabrous Tongues	Monstrous Claws
0-2	10"	2+	5
3-4	8"	2+	4
5-7	6"	3+	4
8-9	6"	4+	4
10-11	4"	5+	3

DESCRIPTION

Morbidex Twiceborn is a single model. He is armed with the deadly Fleshreaper Scythe and rides the belligerent maggoth Tripletongue, which snatches its victims up with its Slabrous Tongues or gores them with its Monstrous Claws.

ABILITIES

Lord of Nurglings: At the start of your hero phase, you can pick 1 friendly Nurglings unit within 7" of Morbidex Twiceborn and add 1 model to it.

Malicious Mites: Add 1 to wound rolls for friendly Nurglings units while they are within 7" of Morbidex Twiceborn.

Nurgle's Rot: At the start of your hero phase, roll a dice for each unit (friend or foe) within 3" of any units with this ability. On the roll of a 6, that unit suffers D3 mortal wounds. Units with the NURGLE keyword are unaffected by this ability.

Repugnant Regrowth: Roll a dice in your hero phase. On a 4+ heal 1 wound that has been allocated to Morbidex Twiceborn. On a 6+ heal D3 wounds instead.

KEYWORDS	CHAOS, MORTAL, NURGLE, ROTBRINGER, MONSTER, HERO, MORBIDEX TWICEBORN

LORD OF AFFLICTIONS

The Lord of Afflictions hovers into battle atop a Rot Fly steed, spearheading the attack of Nurgle's armies. Those foes not crushed or thrown aside by his dolorous tocsin – the enormous wrecking bell strung beneath his steed – are doomed by a stab from his three-pronged festerspike, or else reduced to pools of rancid slurry by the waves of disease that emanate from his incubatch.

MOVE 8"	WOUNDS 8	SAVE 4+	BRAVERY 10

MELEE WEAPONS	Range	Attacks	To Hit	To Wound	Rend	Damage
Festerspike	2"	3	3+	3+	-1	D3
Foul Mouthparts	1"	2	3+	3+	-	1
Venomous Sting	1"	1	4+	3+	-1	D3
Dolorous Tocsin	1"	1	4+	3+	-2	2

DESCRIPTION

A Lord of Afflictions is a single model who carries a Festerspike and rides a Rot Fly that attacks with its Foul Mouthparts, Venomous Sting and the Dolorous Tocsin tethered to its abdomen. Some Lords of Afflictions go into battle with an Incubatch grasped in one hand.

FLY

A Lord of Afflictions can fly.

ABILITIES

Disgustingly Resilient: Roll a dice each time you allocate a wound or mortal wound to this model. On a 5+ the wound is negated.

Rotten Regeneration: At the start of your hero phase, you can heal 1 wound that has been allocated to this model.

Plague Vector: Re-roll hit rolls of 1 for friendly ROTBRINGER units while they are within 7" of this model.

Incubatch: In your hero phase, roll a dice for each unit (friend or foe) within 3" of this model. On a 2+, that unit suffers 1 mortal wound. NURGLE units suffer 1 mortal wound on a 6+ instead.

Virulent Discharge: In your hero phase, roll a dice for each unit (friend or foe) within 3" of any friendly units with this ability. On a 6+ that unit suffers D3 mortal wounds. If the unit has the NURGLE keyword, heal D3 wounds allocated to it instead.

COMMAND ABILITY

Spearhead of Contagion: If this model is your general, you can use this ability in your hero phase. If you do, pick a friendly Pusgoyle Blightlords unit within 14" of this model. Add 8" to that unit's Move characteristic until your next hero phase.

KEYWORDS	CHAOS, MORTAL, DAEMON, NURGLE, ROTBRINGER, HERO, LORD OF AFFLICTIONS

FESTUS THE LEECHLORD

Festus is a heartless maniac, a former plague doctor transformed into a twisted alchemist of disease by the forbidden lore of Nurgle. He leads armies of daemons and rotbringers into battle with infectious ebullience, relishing the chance to try out each new delightful brew upon his unwilling foes and spread bizarre and unnatural plagues swiftly through their ranks.

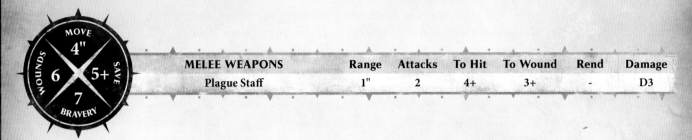

MELEE WEAPONS	Range	Attacks	To Hit	To Wound	Rend	Damage
Plague Staff	1"	2	4+	3+	-	D3

MOVE 4"
WOUNDS 6
SAVE 5+
BRAVERY 7

DESCRIPTION
Festus the Leechlord is a single model. He carries a toxin-laced Plague Staff to battle, and can force doses of his pestilent potions down the throats of his enemies.

ABILITIES
Healing Elixirs: At the start of your hero phase, you can heal 1 wound that has been allocated to Festus the Leechlord.

Delightful Brews, Splendid Restoratives: At the start of your hero phase, you can pick a unit (friend or foe) within 1" of Festus the Leechlord. If you pick a friendly unit, roll a dice. On a 2+ heal D3 wounds that have been allocated to that unit. If you pick an enemy unit, roll a dice. On a 2+ that unit suffers D3 mortal wounds.

MAGIC
Festus the Leechlord is a **WIZARD**. He can attempt to cast one spell in your hero phase, and attempt to unbind one spell in the enemy hero phase. He knows the Arcane Bolt, Mystic Shield and Curse of the Leper spells.

CURSE OF THE LEPER
Curse of the Leper has a casting value of 7. If successfully cast, select a unit within 14" of the caster that is visible to them. Subtract 1 from save rolls for that unit for the rest of the battle. This spell cannot be cast on the same enemy unit more than once during a battle.

KEYWORDS CHAOS, MORTAL, NURGLE, ROTBRINGER, HERO, WIZARD, FESTUS THE LEECHLORD

HARBINGER OF DECAY

Slumped like sacks of flyblown offal in their mouldering saddles, Harbingers of Decay advance into battle atop vile steeds that look more dead than alive. Theirs is the gaze of Nurgle himself, and the mortal worshippers of the Plague God fight all the harder when it falls upon them. Theirs is also the touch of Nurgle, for the slightest cut from their rotswords infects a victim with virulent disease.

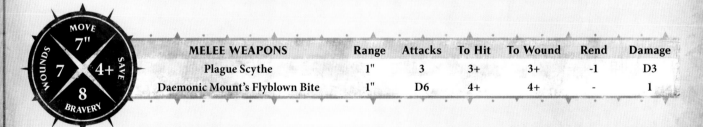

MELEE WEAPONS	Range	Attacks	To Hit	To Wound	Rend	Damage
Plague Scythe	1"	3	3+	3+	-1	D3
Daemonic Mount's Flyblown Bite	1"	D6	4+	4+	-	1

MOVE 7"
WOUNDS 7
SAVE 4+
BRAVERY 8

DESCRIPTION
A Harbinger of Decay is a single model. He wields a Plague Scythe and carries a Rotsword and Soulbound Shield. His emaciated Daemonic Mount spreads diseases with its Flyblown Bite.

ABILITIES
Soulbound Shield: Roll a dice each time you allocate a wound or mortal wound to this model as the result of a spell. On a 4+ the wound is negated.

Rotsword: Once per battle, at the start of your hero phase, pick an enemy **HERO** within 1" of this model and roll a dice. On a 2+ that **HERO** suffers D3 mortal wounds. On a 4+ that **HERO** suffers D3 mortal wounds, and each other enemy unit within 7" of that **HERO** suffers 1 mortal wound.

COMMAND ABILITY
Morbid Vigour: You can use this command ability in your hero phase. If you do, then until your next hero phase roll a dice each time you allocate a wound or mortal wound to a friendly **NURGLE MORTAL** unit while they are within 7" of this model. On a 5+ the wound is negated.

KEYWORDS CHAOS, MORTAL, DAEMON, NURGLE, ROTBRINGER, HERO, HARBINGER OF DECAY

SORCERER

The Sorcerers of Nurgle bring low their enemies with flesh-eating plagues and withering hexes, while shielding their allies with roaring clouds of flies or bloating their bodies with rancid fat to make them all but immune to harm. Some can even vomit streams of unnatural foulness that choke and drown the foe, channelling the foulness of their god to sweep away those who would defy his will.

MELEE WEAPONS	Range	Attacks	To Hit	To Wound	Rend	Damage
Rotwood Staff	2"	1	4+	3+	-1	D3

Stat circle: MOVE 4", WOUNDS 6, SAVE 5+, BRAVERY 7

DESCRIPTION
A Sorcerer is a single model armed with a Rotwood Staff.

ABILITIES
Blessed with Vitality: Roll a dice each time this model successfully casts a spell and it is not unbound. On a 4+ you can heal 1 wound that has been allocated to this model.

MAGIC
A Sorcerer is a **WIZARD**. He can attempt to cast one spell in your hero phase, and attempt to unbind one spell in the enemy hero phase. He knows the Arcane Bolt, Mystic Shield and Stream of Corruption spells.

STREAM OF CORRUPTION
Stream of Corruption has a casting value of 6. If successfully cast, pick an enemy unit that is within 7" of the caster and visible to them. That unit suffers 3 mortal wounds.

KEYWORDS CHAOS, MORTAL, NURGLE, ROTBRINGER, HERO, WIZARD, SORCERER

LORD OF BLIGHTS

The Lord of Blights is a lumbering destroyer who bludgeons his way through the enemy ranks with bubotic hammer and vermid shield. A creator as well as a destroyer, the Lord of Blights cultivates fine crops of death's heads that he hands out to his warriors, enabling them to fling volleys of diseased projectiles. The best of these he keeps, plucking them from his gallowrack to hurl at the foe.

MISSILE WEAPONS	Range	Attacks	To Hit	To Wound	Rend	Damage
Thrice-ripened Death's Head	14"	1	3+	3+	-3	D3
Munificent Bounty Death's Head	14"	1	4+	3+	-	1

MELEE WEAPONS	Range	Attacks	To Hit	To Wound	Rend	Damage
Bubotic Hammer	1"	3	3+	3+	-1	2

Stat circle: MOVE 4", WOUNDS 7, SAVE 4+, BRAVERY 9

DESCRIPTION
A Lord of Blights is a single model. He hurls Thrice-ripened Death's Heads at the enemy and hands out lesser Munificent Bounty Death's Heads for his minions to use. In combat he smashes the foe to the ground with his Bubotic Hammer, while fending off their return blows with his Vermid Shield.

ABILITIES
Munificent Bounty: At the start of your shooting phase, you can pick 1 friendly Putrid Blightkings unit that is within 3" of this model. That unit can shoot in that shooting phase using the Munificent Bounty Death's Head missile weapon shown above.

Vermid Shield: In the combat phase, re-roll save rolls of 1 for this model.

COMMAND ABILITY
Plague of Flies: You can use this command ability in your hero phase. If you do, pick a friendly **NURGLE** unit within 21" of it. Until your next hero phase, subtract 1 from the hit rolls of attacks that target that unit in the shooting phase. If the unit contains 20 or more models, subtract 2 from the hit rolls of attacks that target that unit in the shooting phase, and 1 from the hit rolls of attacks that target that unit in the combat phase instead.

KEYWORDS CHAOS, MORTAL, NURGLE, ROTBRINGER, HERO, LORD OF BLIGHTS

GUTROT SPUME

An arrogant plague lord who destroys all in his path, Gutrot Spume hacks his enemies apart with his corroded axe while entangling, crushing and strangling them with the nest of slimy tentacles that sprouts from his bloated torso. Spume's ego is such that he will never back down from a fight, no matter how terrifying his foe, while his might is such that he rarely loses such duels.

MELEE WEAPONS	Range	Attacks	To Hit	To Wound	Rend	Damage
Rot-pocked Axe	2"	4	3+	2+	-1	2
Flailing Tentacles	1"	D3	2+	4+	-	1

DESCRIPTION
Gutrot Spume is a single model. He is armed with a Rot-pocked Axe and grasps at his foe with a mass of Flailing Tentacles.

ABILITIES
Clutching Pseudopods: At the start of the combat phase, you can pick an enemy model within 1" of Gutrot Spume. Choose a weapon carried by that model and roll a dice. On a 4+ that weapon cannot be used by that model in that combat phase.

Towering Arrogance: Re-roll hit rolls of 1 for Gutrot Spume if the target is a **HERO**. In addition, if Gutrot Spume is within 3" of an enemy **HERO** in the combat phase, he cannot target units that are not **HEROES**.

Master of the Slime Fleet: Instead of setting up Gutrot Spume on the battlefield, you can place him and up to one unit of Putrid Blightkings to one side, and say that they are aboard his flagship. If you do so, at the end of your first movement phase, set up Gutrot Spume and the unit of Putrid Blightkings within 6" of each other, wholly within 6" of the edge of the battlefield and more than 9" from any enemy models.

KEYWORDS CHAOS, MORTAL, NURGLE, ROTBRINGER, HERO, GUTROT SPUME

LORD OF PLAGUES

Infested with myriad diseases, the Lord of Plagues storms into the midst of the enemy army with his rusted axe swinging in measured arcs. This revolting warlord urges his followers on to ever greater acts of carnage, reducing the foe to filth-ridden corpse mulch that will serve to fertilise the Mortal Realms for Nurgle's fecund bounty.

MELEE WEAPONS	Range	Attacks	To Hit	To Wound	Rend	Damage
Plague-ridden Great Blade	1"	3	3+	3+	-1	D3

DESCRIPTION
A Lord of Plagues is a single model. He wields a Plague-ridden Great Blade.

ABILITIES
Wanton Slaughter: Re-roll hit rolls of 1 for friendly Putrid Blightkings units while they are within 7" of this model.

Rotten Corpse Mulch: Roll a dice after this model makes its attacks in the combat phase, and add the number of wounds inflicted by this model (and which were not saved or negated) to the dice roll. If the total is 7+ you immediately receive 1 contagion point.

Plague-ridden Great Weapon: Each time you make a hit roll of 6+ for this model's Plague-ridden Great Blade, that hit roll inflicts D6 hits instead of 1.

COMMAND ABILITY
Grandfather's Gift: You can use this command ability in your hero phase. If you do, pick an enemy unit within 21" of it and roll 7 dice. That unit suffers 1 mortal wound for each roll of 6+.

KEYWORDS CHAOS, MORTAL, NURGLE, ROTBRINGER, HERO, LORD OF PLAGUES

PUTRID BLIGHTKINGS

Hulking warriors of Nurgle, the Putrid Blightkings carve their way through the enemy with slime-encrusted axes, hammers and flails. Their rotting bodies can absorb tremendous amounts of punishment, allowing the Blightkings to drive relentlessly through the foe's battle line and shatter it apart, before hacking down the survivors with contemptuous ease.

MOVE 4" | WOUNDS 4 | SAVE 4+ | BRAVERY 8

MELEE WEAPONS	Range	Attacks	To Hit	To Wound	Rend	Damage
Blighted Weapon	1"	3	3+	3+	-	1

DESCRIPTION
A unit of Putrid Blightkings has 5 or more models, armed with a variety of filth-encrusted Blighted Weapons.

BLIGHTLORD
The leader of this unit is a Blightlord. A Blightlord has a Wounds characteristic of 5.

ICON BEARERS
Models in this unit may be Icon Bearers. Add 1 to this unit's Bravery characteristic while it includes any Icon Bearers.

SONOROUS TOCSIN
Models in this unit may carry a Sonorous Tocsin. Add 1 to this unit's run and charge rolls whilst it includes any models carrying a Sonorous Tocsin.

ABILITIES
Virulent Discharge: In your hero phase, roll a dice for each unit (friend or foe) that is within 3" of any friendly units with this ability. On a 6+ that unit suffers D3 mortal wounds. If the unit has the NURGLE keyword, heal D3 wounds allocated to the unit instead.

Blighted Weapons: Each time you make a hit roll of 6+ for this unit's Blighted Weapons, that hit roll inflicts D6 hits instead of 1.

KEYWORDS | CHAOS, MORTAL, NURGLE, ROTBRINGER, PUTRID BLIGHTKINGS

PUSGOYLE BLIGHTLORDS

Elite Rotbringers mounted atop bloated Rot Flies, the Pusgoyle Blightlords thrum ahead of the armies of Nurgle to sow panic and death. Their dolorous tocsins smash through the enemy ranks as they thrum overhead, while their whistling scythes reap heads from necks like crops ripe for the harvest.

MOVE 8" | WOUNDS 7 | SAVE 4+ | BRAVERY 8

MELEE WEAPONS	Range	Attacks	To Hit	To Wound	Rend	Damage
Blighted Weapon	1"	3	3+	3+	-	1
Dolorous Tocsin	1"	1	4+	3+	-2	2
Foul Mouthparts	1"	2	3+	3+	-	1
Venomous Sting	1"	1	4+	3+	-1	D3

DESCRIPTION
A unit of Pusgoyle Blightlords has any number of models. The Rot Flies stab the enemy with Venomous Stings, and bite with Foul Mouthparts. Their Blightlord riders attack using a variety of filth-encrusted Blighted Weapons. Up to half of the models in this unit can be armed with a weighty bell known as a Dolorous Tocsin in addition to their other weapons.

FLY
Pusgoyle Blightlords can fly.

ABILITIES
Disgustingly Resilient: Roll a dice each time you allocate a wound or mortal wound to a model in this unit. On a 5+ the wound is negated.

Virulent Discharge: In your hero phase, roll a dice for each unit (friend or foe) that is within 3" of any friendly units with this ability. On a 6+ that unit suffers D3 mortal wounds. If the unit has the NURGLE keyword, heal D3 wounds allocated to the unit instead.

Blighted Weapons: Each time you make a hit roll of 6+ for this unit's Blighted Weapons, that hit roll inflicts D6 hits instead of 1.

KEYWORDS | CHAOS, MORTAL, DAEMON, NURGLE, ROTBRINGER, PUSGOYLE BLIGHTLORDS

FECULENT GNARLMAW

Wherever the servants of Nurgle gather in large numbers and the blessed rot begins to set in, Feculent Gnarlmaws push their way up through the blighted soil. These disgusting trees ring with the sorrowful tolling of entropic chimes, belch clouds of daemonic spores, and shed rot-wet blossom to carpet the maggot-churned earth beneath their boughs.

DESCRIPTION
A Feculent Gnarlmaw is a terrain feature consisting of 1 Feculent Gnarlmaw scenery model.

SCENERY RULES
The following scenery rules are used for this terrain feature (do not roll on the Scenery Table on the *Warhammer Age of Sigmar* rules sheet).

Entropic Chimes: In their charge phase, **NURGLE** units that are within 7" of any Feculent Gnarlmaws can attempt to charge even if they ran in the same turn.

Sickness Blossoms: At the start of the hero phase, roll a dice for each unit within 3" of any Feculent Gnarlmaws. On a 4+ the unit suffers 1 mortal wound. Units with the **NURGLE** keyword are unaffected by this ability.

KEYWORDS	SCENERY, FECULENT GNARLMAW

PITCHED BATTLE PROFILES

The tables below provide points, minimum and maximum unit sizes and battlefield roles for the warscrolls and warscroll battalions in this book, for use in Pitched Battles. Used alongside the rules for Pitched Battles in the *General's Handbook*, this provides you with everything you need to field your Nurgle army in a Pitched Battle against any opponent.

MAGGOTKIN OF NURGLE UNIT	UNIT SIZE MIN	MAX	POINTS	BATTLEFIELD ROLE	NOTES
Plaguebearers	10	30	120/320	Battleline	
Epidemius, Tallyman of Nurgle	1	1	200	Leader	Only one of this model can be included in a Pitched Battle army.
Festus the Leechlord	1	1	140	Leader	Only one of this model can be included in a Pitched Battle army.
Gutrot Spume	1	1	140	Leader	Only one of this model can be included in a Pitched Battle army.
Harbinger of Decay	1	1	160	Leader	
Horticulous Slimux	1	1	220	Leader	Only one of this model can be included in a Pitched Battle army.
Lord of Afflictions	1	1	220	Leader	
Lord of Blights	1	1	140	Leader	
Lord of Plagues	1	1	140	Leader	
Poxbringer, Herald of Nurgle	1	1	120	Leader	
Sloppity Bilepiper, Herald of Nurgle	1	1	100	Leader	
Spoilpox Scrivener, Herald of Nurgle	1	1	100	Leader	
Sorcerer	1	1	120	Leader	
Bloab Rotspawned	1	1	260	Leader, Behemoth	Only one of this model can be included in a Pitched Battle army.
Great Unclean One	1	1	340	Leader, Behemoth	
Morbidex Twiceborn	1	1	260	Leader, Behemoth	Only one of this model can be included in a Pitched Battle army.
Orghotts Daemonspew	1	1	260	Leader, Behemoth	Only one of this model can be included in a Pitched Battle army.
Rotigus	1	1	340	Leader, Behemoth	Only one of this model can be included in a Pitched Battle army.
The Glottkin	1	1	420	Leader, Behemoth	Only one of this model can be included in a Pitched Battle army.
Beasts of Nurgle	1	6	100		
Nurglings	3	12	100		
Plague Drones	3	12	200		
Pusgoyle Blightlords	2	12	220		Battleline if army has NURGLE allegiance and general is a Lord of Afflictions.
Putrid Blightkings	5	20	160/580		Battleline if army has NURGLE allegiance.
Affliction Cyst	-	-	220	*Warscroll Battalion*	
Blight Cyst	-	-	220	*Warscroll Battalion*	
Plague Cyst	-	-	220	*Warscroll Battalion*	
The Munificent Wanderers	-	-	180	*Warscroll Battalion*	
Nurgle's Menagerie	-	-	240	*Warscroll Battalion*	
Tallyband of Nurgle	-	-	220	*Warscroll Battalion*	
Thricefold Befoulment	-	-	160	*Warscroll Battalion*	
The Blessed Sons	-	-	200	*Warscroll Battalion*	

Nurgle Allies: Khorne, Brayherds, Chaos Gargants, Everchosen, Monsters of Chaos, Slaanesh, Slaves to Darkness (excluding units with mark of Tzeentch), Warherds

SCENERY UNIT	UNIT SIZE MIN	MAX	POINTS	BATTLEFIELD ROLE	NOTES
Feculent Gnarlmaw	1	1	0	Scenery